Solving a Retirement Dilemma

*Spend Less or
Run Out of Money*

**How to Spend More
Live the Lifestyle You Deserve
Make it Last a Lifetime**

James Schweinsburg

Copyrighted Material

Copyright and Disclaimer

Solving a Retirement Dilemma – *Spend Less or Run out of Money* - How to Spend More - Live the Lifestyle You Deserve Make It Last a Lifetime

Copyright © 2020 by James Schweinsburg.
All Rights Reserved.

No part of this publication may be reproduced, stored or transmitted in any form or by any means, electronic, mechanical, photocopying, recording, scanning or otherwise, except as permitted under Section 107 or 108 of the 1976 United States Copyright Act, without the prior written permission of the author. Requests for permission should be addressed to **retirementdilemma@outlook.com**

The worksheets contained in this book can be reproduced without the prior written permission of the author if it is for personal use only.

Although the author and publisher have used their best efforts in preparing this book, they make no representations or warranties with respect to the accuracy or completeness of its contents. The advice contained in this book may not be suitable for your situation. It is sold with the understanding that the author or publisher are not engaged in providing any professional advice or services. You should consult with a professional where appropriate. Neither the publisher or author shall be liable for any loss of profit or any other damages, including but not limited to special, incidental, or consequential damages.

ISBN-13: 979-8637728152
Independently published   First Edition

Preface

After the success of my first book which was a step by step workbook titled **Spend More Money in Retirement** *It May be More than You Think*, I was encouraged by the feedback and positive reviews to write a greatly expanded version. This allowed me to widen the focus from that of a step by step workbook and include significantly more information on what you need to know in creating and executing a successful retirement plan. *One that will allow you to achieve the Lifestyle you deserve.*

The main purpose of this book is to share what I learned through both extensive reading and research on retirement investing and financial planning, and my experiences in planning for and living in retirement the past several years. *My hope is that this book will give you the knowledge and confidence to spend more of what you earned, live the retirement lifestyle you deserve, and make it last your lifetime.*

I also hope to provide you with a solution to what I believe is the most significant dilemma facing retirees, either to **Spend Less** or **Run out of Money**. You will learn that underspending is not a very precise or rewarding method of making your money last.

The title of this book was chosen after reading about how many retirees underspend in retirement possibly depriving themselves of a more enjoyable retirement.

There are many reasons for this, maybe some psychological and some behavioral, but not knowing how much can be safely spent without outliving retirement savings, is a significant obstacle. This book will show you how.

Why is this book different from the many books written on this subject? First, I am not a professional Financial Planner or Investment Adviser. I am a retired executive and engineer, trained and experienced in analyzing and solving difficult problems. I have learned many valuable lessons in preparing for and living in retirement. I believe this allows me to bring a fresh perspective and simplification to this complex subject.

Second, it is not just another retirement planning book that explains all the complexities of the issues facing retirees, explains their advantages and disadvantages, but then leaves you without specific recommendations or an actual executable plan. My goal is not to convince you to agree with me or my conclusions but rather to induce critical thought for each of the topics and positions covered in this book.

Third, this book will not try to get you to buy additional services or publications like many financial books and authors attempt to do.

I began thinking about retirement issues many years before actually retiring. Among my first questions were, **what retirement Lifestyle did we want to have** *and what would it look like*? This led to the next question, **how much money would we need to support the lifestyle we envisioned in retirement**?

As I quickly discovered, answering these questions was no easy task and it led me to seek the answer to another critical question; ***If you need or want to spend more than your retirement income, how much savings could be safely withdrawn each year so that you do not outlive your savings?*** The answers to these and many more questions are provided by this book.

You cannot predict the future with certainty, but this book will help you make the decisions and calculations you need to make to determine if your planned lifestyle is achievable.

If you choose to work with a financial planner or advisor, hopefully this book will provide you with valuable information on selecting, working with, and measuring their performance.

Acknowledgement

I would like to give a special thanks to those that purchased my first book and took the time to provide valuable feedback and encouragement. To my loving wife Cecilia, who's love, support and inspiration gave me the motivation to keep working on this book and documenting the many retirement issues and decisions we faced along with the successes, failures, and mistakes we made along the way.

Table of Contents

Introduction	**11**
1 **What will Your Retirement Look Like?**	**18**
Do You Fear Retiring?	19
Are you Afraid to Spend?	20
Where will you Live in Retirement?	22
2 **What will it Cost?**	**32**
How will your Spending change with age?	33
Some Cost Items to Consider	35
Covering Emergencies	40
Budgeting Suggestions	40
Worksheet 1: Establish your Desired Spending	44
3 **Your Expected Income**	**46**
When to take Social Security Benefits	47
When delaying does not make sense	52
You can change your mind	53
The Income Tax Surprises!	56
Should you buy an Annuity?	57
Worksheet 2: Expected Annual After-Tax Income	67

4 Do You have enough Saved? — 68
    Your Retirement Number — 69
    Should you Work Longer? — 71
    Worksheet 3: Total Spendable Value of Your Savings — 73

5 Test Drive Your Retirement Decisions — 74

6 Navigating the Risks to your Retirement Plan — 78
    The Risk of Long-Term Care — 79
    The Greatest Risk to your Retirement Plan — 80

7 Will you need a Financial Advisor or Planner? — 85
    What to Look For — 89
    How to Measure your Financial Advisor's Performance — 91
    How to Measure your Financial Planner's Performance — 92
    Advisor Fees — 94

8 A Better System of Spending Your Savings — 98
    The 4% Withdrawal System — 100
    The 1/N Withdrawal System — 104
    The RMD Withdrawal System — 106
    The Variable Percentage Withdrawal System — 108

9 Compare Savings Withdrawal Systems — 111

Total withdrawn over 30 years	**112**
Amount of Savings after 30 years	**113**
Withdrawals in the early years versus later years	**115**
Key Takeaways	**116**
10 Set Spending Limits	**122**
Setting Lower & Upper Spending Limits	**123**
Creating a separate reserve fund	**124**
11 Calculate Your Safe Withdrawal Amount	**127**
How long do you want your plan to last?	**128**
Worksheet 4: Using the 4% System	**132**
Worksheet 5: Using the 1/N System	**136**
Worksheet 6: Using the RMD System	**140**
Worksheet 7: Using the VPW System	**145**
12 Opportunities to Reduce Spending	**150**
Should You Downsize?	**150**
13 Minimizing Taxes & Maximizing Investment Returns	**157**
What type of assets to Sell?	**157**
In what order should you withdraw?	**159**
Consider Rolling Over Your 401K	**162**
Why consider a Roth IRA?	**164**

Do You Have an HSA account?	168
14 Investing for Growth	**170**
Avoiding, Managing, or Transferring Risk	170
Where to put your investments	173
The importance of Asset Allocation	175
The Importance of Rebalancing Assets	177
The importance of reducing investment fees	178
15 How will you handle a Major Market Downturn?	**181**
16 Investing for Peace of Mind	**185**
What is the Bucket Strategy?	185
17 How is Your Retirement Plan Doing?	**192**
Your Checklist	193
18 Summary	**197**
Appendix I: Estimating Your Income Taxes	**203**
Appendix II: Keeping Track	**209**
Appendix III: Financial Data	**210**
Appendix IV: References and Resources	**212**
Afterword	**214**

Introduction

Retirement can be rewarding, exciting, and challenging, bringing new experiences as well as uncertainties. It is a chance to design a lifestyle that incorporates many of your interests and dreams.

Building a detailed plan for your retirement will be vital to how successful your retirement will be. Creating a retirement income, spending, and investing plan requires, among other things:

- Deciding on the retirement Lifestyle you want.

- Creating a spending budget that supports your retirement lifestyle.

- Understanding the trade-off between spending money in the early years of retirement against saving money for your later years.

- Deciding when to take Social Security benefits.

- Understanding how taxes in retirement will reduce your income.

- Should you buy an annuity and when?

- Estimating how long you will live or at least how long you want your savings to last.

- Choosing a savings withdrawal system that you are most comfortable with and will last as-long-as you do.

- Navigating the many risks to your retirement.

- Deciding what savings and investment accounts to withdraw from and in what order to minimize taxes and maximize investment returns.

- Choosing Where and How Much to invest in stocks, bonds and cash for safety, diversification, investment growth to protect against inflation, and most importantly safety and peace of mind.

Your retirement plan should include:

Guaranteed Income such as Social security, Pensions, and possibly Annuities, that will cover your fixed and essential non-discretionary expenses like food, housing, transportation, and health care.

Growth potential to meet long-term needs and offset the impact of inflation. How much should you invest in Cash, Bonds, and Stocks?

Spending Flexibility especially for your non-essential discretionary spending and to be able to adjust spending and refine your plan as needed over time.

The chapters that follow will provide answers and suggestions for addressing these and other issues you may be faced with on your retirement journey.

How this book is organized

I tried to write this book in a logical progression to make it easier to follow along and create your retirement plan. It includes many topics that we found useful in creating and executing our own retirement plan.

Chapter 1 is where you determine the *Lifestyle you would like to have* in retirement.

Chapter 2 begins to address what it might cost to achieve the lifestyle you envisioned and focuses on creating a *Desirable Spending Budget*. Worksheet 1 at the end of the chapter is included to help you create it, and although it may or may not be achievable, you will have a chance later to revise it.

Chapter 3 looks at your expected sources of retirement income and includes worksheet 2 to capture it. It will look at opportunities to increase the amount of guaranteed income you can receive for life and thus reduce the amount you may need to withdraw from savings, especially later in retirement when you may need it the most.

Chapter 4 will begin to address the question "How much savings do we need to have to support the retirement Lifestyle we want to have?" It includes worksheet 3 to capture the portion of your savings and investments you plan to spend to help support your retirement lifestyle.

Chapter 5 will discuss the many important retirement decisions that you should test drive before it is too late or too costly to undo.

Chapter 6 will look at the significant risks that your retirement plan may encounter and some suggestions to address them.

Chapter 7 addresses whether you may need help and advice to build a sustainable retirement plan, how to choose the right help, how to measure their performance, and what it may cost.

Chapter 8 looks at four completely different savings withdrawal systems each designed to prevent you from outliving your savings. They are the most thoroughly tested and most often recommended systems by financial planners.

Chapter 9 will compare the advantages and disadvantages of the four savings withdrawal systems and help you choose the system you are most comfortable with in funding your retirement.

Chapter 10 explores the advantages of setting upper and lower spending limits around your spending plan. It also explains an option to create a reserve fund instead of setting spending limits.

Chapter 11 is the chapter where you will choose the savings withdrawal system you are most comfortable using and then calculate what your annual safe withdrawal and safe spending amounts are.

Chapter 12 will explore the many opportunities to reduce spending if needed or desired. It may allow you to shift expenses to more valuable and rewarding expenditures and reduce unnecessary expenses.

Chapter 13 will discuss why it is important to decide which accounts you should withdraw from and in what order when you need to fund your retirement.

Chapter 14 focuses on the importance of investing for growth. It will look at dealing with investment risk, where you should locate your investments, how they should be allocated for growth, and the importance of keeping those allocations in balance over time.

Chapter 15 looks at the question "How will you handle a major market downturn?". Hopefully, the issues and ideas presented will prevent you from making significant mistakes with your investments.

Chapter 16 talks about a unique method of positioning your investments for safety and peace of mind especially when market downturns happen.

Chapter 17 addresses the importance of reviewing how well your retirement plan is doing and provides an annual checklist.

Chapter 18 is where I summarize all the key takeaways from the previous chapters with examples of how we have incorporated them into our retirement plan.

Long before thinking about writing this book, I researched many different savings withdrawal systems and created a computerized spreadsheet program to help me plan for my retirement and help me organize my thoughts. I wanted a computer program that allowed me to calculate the effects of a variety of what-if scenarios and help me choose a savings withdrawal system that I would be most comfortable with. I wanted a program that could analyze various spending budgets, determine how much could be safely withdrawn from available savings (without running out of money under various time horizons), and help track progress.

The current version of the spreadsheet program is available for free when you purchase this book. It includes the necessary worksheets and automates much of the data input and number crunching, saving you time. It has gone through many revisions and improvements in the years since it was created.

For those of you who are familiar with computer spreadsheets, I urge you to get it before you start using the worksheets. For those of you not familiar with spreadsheets, I created a pdf file containing all the worksheets and tables so you can print them out and use them each year. See the Afterword section at the end of this book on how to get them.

CAUTION: The future may contain scenarios that are better or worse than anything considered by this book. It is also important to remember that, despite the sophistication of the methods used, this book makes several simplifying assumptions. Note that the Suggested Withdrawal amounts are just that, Suggestions, and are designed to prevent you from significantly over or under spending your savings. It is recommended that you seek additional guidance in developing a retirement plan with which you will be most comfortable.

Chapter 1

What will Your Retirement Look Like?

In this chapter we will focus on helping you determine what Lifestyle will make you and your spouse or partner **Happy.** You know what you are retiring *from* but what are you retiring *to*? Focus on the big picture first. Chapter 2 is where you will determine what your **Desired** Lifestyle will cost and in later chapters whether it is achievable, and if not, what adjustments will be needed. But for now, try to think of the life you *want* to live instead of the life you *had* to live while working. Try to create a clear vision of what your retirement Lifestyle might look like.

You typically have only one shot at retiring correctly, so, do not jump into the decisions too quickly. You would not think to buy a new car without test driving it, so why would you make critical retirement decisions without a test drive? In chapter 5 we will discuss the many important retirement decisions that you should test drive before you implement them.

Keep in mind that a happy and successful retirement is much more than just financial issues. It is about creating an active and purposeful retirement that includes family, friends, interesting leisure activities, creative endeavors, as well as physical and mental health pursuits. Many retirees without purpose and something to keep active wind up depressed and bored. Many also experience a rapid decline in both mental and physical health soon after retiring or after their bucket list is completed.

Do You Fear Retiring?

Those of you that have a strong work ethic and never slowed down from work may fear retiring because you do not know what you will do after retiring. To some degree many people worry about not having enough money or leaving the sense of comradery and engagement offered by working. Others worry about how they will fill all the newfound time they will have.

All too often people fear retirement because they focus on what they are giving up instead of focusing on what they are gaining. You might not expect boredom to be a big threat to your retirement, but many retirees say it can be, especially after the first couple of years when you have completed many of your bucket list items.

Merrill Lynch has found that seniors who give back in some way, whether volunteering or contributing to organizations whose values and goals they support, were more likely to say they were happier and had a strong sense of purpose in life.

Think about doing activities where you can use your knowledge, skills, or experience, and have some fun doing it. The payback can be far more than purely financial. "The activity of working, of using your brain, of interacting with others is extremely valuable for your health and your happiness," says Steven Feinschreiber, senior vice president of research in Fidelity's Financial Solutions, Inc. "Research suggests that working can actually help you live a longer and healthier life."

Are you Afraid to Spend?

You would think that having a great time spending all the money you have put away for retirement, would be easy. After all, the whole point of saving and investing during your working years is to have the money to enjoy after you stop working.

But several recent studies suggest that many people may have a harder time spending down their retirement nest egg than you might think. For example, a 2016 study of retiree spending habits found that with the exception of those of modest means, retirees on average were spending less than they could actually afford, while wealthy retirees were spending less than half of the amount their savings would support.

In 2019 when researchers for the BlackRock Retirement Institute examined the spending and savings of thousands of people who retired in the early 1990s, they not only found that most of these retirees still had at least half of their retirement savings remaining after nearly 20 years of retirement, but that many actually had a larger amount than when they began retirement.

There can be several explanations for this reluctance to spend down one's retirement savings:

- Some are being cautious because they fear they might have large medical expenses late in life or that they will run through their savings too early and must cut expenses or make sacrifices later in life.

- Others may simply have trouble making the transition from saving to spending. After years of being thrifty to increase their savings, they have developed an extreme reluctance to spend, which makes it difficult to be less thrifty in retirement when they need to start drawing down those savings. They never get to enjoy the benefits of all those years of saving provides.

- Some retirees, especially those with a considerable amount of money saved, may plan on leaving a portion of their savings to their heirs or favorite causes.

- But for many retires, not knowing how much can be safely spent without outliving retirement savings, is a significant obstacle. They may lack the knowledge and confidence of using a savings withdrawal system that is designed to maximize their savings withdrawals while having those savings last as-long-as they choose.

Chapters 8 and 9 will expose you to some savings withdrawal systems that can help you maximize your retirement spending while making your savings last a lifetime.

Where will you Live in Retirement?

One of the great benefits that retirement provides is the opportunity to choose where you want to live. Instead of living near where you work, you can choose to live in a place that offers the surroundings and climate that will allow you to enjoy your retirement to its fullest.

Will you continue to live in the same home where you raised a family and built a career? Will you move to a retirement community where you can bond with other active seniors and enjoy all the activities they can provide? Will you sell your home and use the money to hit the road, perhaps buying an RV and driving across the country?

The answer to these questions can have a major impact not only on your finances but on your retirement happiness. Choosing to move presents an opportunity to completely relocate and experience a new lifestyle. Many retirees dream of moving to a warmer climate, one where there is no snow to shovel or icy roads to drive on. If your current climate is too hot, too cold, too humid, or too dry, you can pick a new place that accommodates the lifestyle you envision.

Selling your home may improve your quality of life and give you more time to pursue hobbies and other interests. You may have needed that large home when you were raising your children, but now that they are grown and out on their own, all that space just means more cleaning and upkeep.

Some Important Criteria to Consider:

About one million people move every year after they retire. Some people move to be closer to or farther away from family while others for health or financial reasons. Many of the criteria you will use to select your ideal retirement location are obvious, such as the cost of living, taxes, safety, and climate. However, there are many other important criteria to consider that might be less obvious.

Here are some qualities you should evaluate when you are looking at potential retirement destinations:

- *What Amenities are most important in supporting your desired lifestyle?* Think about the activities that are most important to you and your partner, then investigate if the area you are considering offers enough of them. For example, if you enjoy fine dining, look at what the local restaurant scene offers. If you are used to having a Costco or a Trader Joe's nearby, could you be happy in an area where these stores are not close enough? The same for, museums, theaters, live music, adult education classes hiking trails, golf courses, gyms and more.

- *Do you want to move near or away from your children?* While you may love your kids and grandkids you may be tired of providing endless free childcare. If you are moving to be closer, will they stay put or will they eventually move to a distant city for work, leaving you alone in an unfamiliar town after leaving behind your friends and the comfort of a familiar location. Keep in mind that technology such as FaceTime and Skype have made it easier to stay in touch.

- *Do you value opportunities to socialize?* An active social life is one of the most important components of a happy retirement. If you prefer to socialize with other retirees, you may want to move to an active adult community or live in a city that has a large senior population. If you prefer to socialize with people who have similar interests to yours, you can read local publications to get a feel for what social opportunities are available.

- *The ability to age in place.* When the time comes to buy or rent a new home, choose one that will serve you well as you get older. A one-story home may be advisable, but will you be able to navigate if you need to use a walker or wheelchair someday. You should consider how large a home you are willing to maintain and the amount of yard maintenance you are willing to do, both now and in the future.

- *Quality of health care facilities.* When you begin your retirement, you will probably be healthy and active. But in your later years, the availability of good doctors, quality hospitals, affordable assisted living facilities, and nursing homes will become critical. As you age, it will be more difficult to relocate to find better health care options. You should spend the time to investigate the services that are available in the area you are considering.

- *Cost of health insurance.* If you retire before you become eligible for Medicare or if you will not have employer-provided health insurance, then you will need to purchase your health insurance on the open market until you become eligible for Medicare. The cost of health insurance and the number of choices varies widely from state to state especially if you qualify for a government subsidy and will be buying your health insurance on your state's health care exchange. You should research the costs and levels of coverage provided by the insurance plans that will be available at your new location.

- *How important is moving to an area that offers great views?* Locations with gorgeous scenery or waterfront often have a higher cost of living. Living on or near coastal areas comes with the potential for catastrophic storms, flooding, and extremely high home-owners insurance. You might find popular locations are not worth the traffic or invasion of tourists. If you do find yourself regretting the decision, reversing it could be difficult and expensive.

- *Proximity to a major airport.* If you plan to travel, you will most likely appreciate living within a reasonable drive from an airport that offers regular flights to many destinations. Having to drive several hours in addition to the time spent on an airplane or having to make extra connections will make your travel more tiring, and it will be more costly to take a cab or shuttle and more difficult to have friends take you to the airport. Also, if you expect to entertain visitors and family members, living closer to an airport will make life easier.

- *Signs of future prosperity or decline.* The town or neighborhood you are considering might look good Today but try to envision how it will look in the distant future. A lot can happen, but there are several signs you can look for. If the local economy is strong and the major employers are in industries with a promising future, that is a strong indicator that the city will prosper. On the other hand, a heavy concentration of aging manufacturing plants is less promising. You can observe whether there is a lot of new building and revitalization of existing neighborhoods or if homes are falling into disrepair, or shopping centers have many vacant stores.

Retirement is a major change in terms of finances, but the change in lifestyle is just as significant. If selling your home and possibly downsizing in retirement is something you are willing to consider, doing the research and testing it out by renting for a few months may help you avoid a costly mistake.

Here are some additional housing options to consider:

Stay at Home: Most people age 50 and older (77 percent) want to stay at or near where they are, for as long as possible, according to the 2018 Home and Community Preferences survey by AARP. If you are comfortable at home, involved in your current neighborhood activities or regularly host get togethers, remaining at your current home might make sense.

In some cases, emotional ties can make selling your home difficult. That home is, where you raised your family and made close friends. You may find that you would regret selling a home with such a strong emotional attachment.

Is your current home capable of letting you age in place, especially if you become disabled? Your home may need changes to accommodate health needs as you age. You might have to make expensive home renovations to put in ramps, a ground floor bedroom or change the bathroom design to make it more accessible. If you need help with daily activities, you may have to bring in family members or a nurse.

Move to a Retirement Community: Rather than staying at home, you might opt for an active adult community, assisted living facility or continuing care retirement community. Each may offer benefits to retirees to assist with living, although it is important to consider each option based on the retiree's current health. You might choose a place where you can live independently but have the option of more care later.

Many retirement communities offer amenities like a pool, gym, fitness classes, craft activities, learning opportunities, and social events. You may also find services like lawn care, home maintenance and food preparation available in many places. Most 55 plus retirement developments have homes or condos that are designed to make it easier to age in place with barrier free access.

Always check the fine print. Many facilities ask you to make an upfront payment and then ongoing monthly installments. Some may have rules that you may find are too restrictive.

Move to a Condo: If you want to live in a location that is close to restaurants, theaters, shopping, and learning opportunities, a condo might be a good fit. Many condos are located within walking distance to restaurants and entertainment. You also might get amenities like pool access, yard maintenance and house upkeep. If you currently live in a large home, you might find a smaller space easier to manage.

Read the rules carefully before making a move, as condos usually come with many restrictions and require you to pay monthly association dues. However, the dues may represent good value and include costs you would normally pay extra for.

Renting: If your current home is getting harder to keep up, renting could be a good choice. If you rent, you will not be responsible for maintenance like lawn care and snow removal. You will also have predictable housing costs, as you will not be responsible for most repairs.

However, renting in a popular urban area with a rising cost of living could bring unexpected costs. You could find the rent increasing after a year and reaches an amount you can no longer afford.

It is always a good idea to rent in a new locale before you make any long-term commitments. This will allow you to determine whether you are going to enjoy the area and give you time to discover more about the local housing market. You would not want to relocate a long distance away only to realize how much you miss your family or your family needs you closer.

A word about Fee Simple versus Leasehold Home Ownership. If you plan to move to Florida, Hawaii, or New York you will need to understand the difference between fee simple and leasehold ownership. The most common form of home ownership is fee simple giving the owner full possession of the property when they buy it.

However, the states mentioned above have both fee simple and leasehold ownership. While most of the state's leasehold single-family properties have converted to fee simple ownership over the past few decades, the leasehold option remains alive in the condo market. For most homebuyers, they are not a good option, but there are reasons leasehold properties might be at least worthy of your due diligence: affordability, the right fit for some lifestyles and an income opportunity.

The first difference with leasehold is that the lessee does not own the land, but only has the right to use it for a predetermined amount of time. The second difference is if the leasehold property is sold, the lessee will only have the use of the property for the remaining years of the lease. At the end of the lease period, the land reverts to the lessor.

Depending on how the lease is written and how the surrender clause in it is stated, buildings and any other improvements made, may also revert to the lessor. This is a reason to be overly cautious since the resale value and your equity may decrease as it gets closer to the land lease expiring. Usually, buildings depreciate, and the land appreciates in value.

Remember, it is up to you to design a retirement lifestyle that is as invigorating yet relaxing as you want it to be. You must find those things that matter most to you. To do more of what you like to do and less of what you do not.

Chapter 2

What will it Cost?

After you have determined the Lifestyle you would like to have in retirement you need to have an idea of what it will cost, in order to know if you can afford it. It is important to start your retirement with a spending plan that works for you.

For those of you that have been using a budgeting system for some time and have a pretty good idea on what your retirement budget might look like, I recommend continuing to read this chapter for thoughts and ideas that may alter your retirement budget thinking.

For those that do not have a budgeting system, I know the word – BUDGETING conjures up all kinds of groaning and moaning. But it really does not have to be that painful. Making a spending budget each year may not be the first thing you look forward to, but it is one of the most important things you can do to start your retirement on the right path.

Along with an income plan that can deliver a steady retirement paycheck and an investing strategy that allows a portion of your savings the chance to grow, a realistic spending budget is an essential cornerstone of a successful retirement.

Worksheet 1 at the end of this chapter is where you will create your *desired* annual spending budget. It might be a good idea to start filling it out as you read through this chapter, unless you already have a good budgeting system you would prefer to use. Remember that you are creating your desired spending budget and although it may not be achievable, you will have an opportunity to revise it after completing chapter 11.

One more thing you can do to increase your odds of having a happier and more rewarding retirement is to spend it in ways that have been shown to generate more satisfaction and happiness for retirees. Some research suggests that only one type of spending predicted retirement satisfaction, the money spent on leisure activities, including travel, entertainment, dining out and hobbies. Such spending tends to boost happiness because it keeps us more active and socially engaged.

How will your spending change with age?

Popular belief is that your spending will increase as you age due to inflation and the rising costs of health care, but some studies suggest otherwise. Data from the Bureau of Labor Statistics suggests the opposite is true. It shows that spending tends to peak at age 55 and then for every 10 years after, it drops approximately 10 to 14%. Although healthcare expenses nearly double during this period, almost all other expenses steadily decline. The big question mark is the amount of travel and leisure expenses you will incur in the first few years of retirement when you have newfound time on your hands and a bucket list you want to pursue. In these cases, your retirement spending may go up in the first few years before declining.

As an example, for someone who is age 55-65 and needs $60,000 to cover their annual living expenses, the BLS numbers suggest that they will likely need $52,800, between age 65-75, and then $46,500 after age 75 (assuming today's dollars). The BLS numbers do not suggest that there will not be inflation experienced during retirement, but rather that we simply buy fewer things.

When thinking about retirement possibly lasting 30 or more years, I believe, as many financial planners do, that there are three retirement phases that most retirees will go through. The age that each phase starts and ends of course is dependent to a large extent on the retiree's health. I like to think of them as:

- **The Bucket List phase** when you are most active with newfound time on your hands and lots of things you want to see and do.

- **The Let's Relax phase** where you have completed most of your bucket list and are physically starting to slow down.

- **Homebound phase** where most discretionary expenses disappear, and your largest expense may be health related.

Some Cost items to Consider

If you are not yet in retirement and do not have a good understanding of what it will cost to have the lifestyle you want in retirement, the following may help. Remember, you most likely will have more time in retirement to enjoy more activities which may require you to spend more on travel, entertainment, and leisure activities.

Keep in mind that the goal should be to create as flexible a retirement lifestyle as possible, keeping your fixed and necessary expenditures as low as possible to allow for more discretionary spending when your investments perform well or to reduce discretionary spending when your investments perform poorly in any given year. As you will see in subsequent chapters, I cannot stress enough how important this is, to achieving a satisfying and rewarding retirement.

Your home: Where will you live? Changing your housing or moving can significantly increase or decrease your expenses. Even if you plan to remain in the same house, some of your costs will still change. For example, your utility bills may increase if you spend more time at home. Or they may decrease if you spend more time traveling away from home.

As your home ages you may spend more on repairs and maintenance. A good rule of thumb is to budget at least 1% of your home's value for annual maintenance. So, if your home is worth $300,000, then budget approximately $3,000 per year for standard repairs, general upkeep, or accessibility upgrades.

Transportation: What does it cost you now? How might it change in retirement? No longer having commuting costs is a bonus, but your transportation costs will not stop. Most people do not retire to sit around the house, so remember to include the cost of gas, auto insurance and vehicle maintenance expenses. Do you really need two cars? If you are considering buying a new or used car, you will need to budget that as well.

Food: Will you eat out more often in retirement, or entertain friends and family more often? Will you spend less because you no longer buy lunches or other food items at work or will you want to cook more often? Several studies have suggested that your overall expenditures on food will not change significantly when you retire.

Travel: How you budget for travel will depend on the types of trips you are planning and how extensive your bucket list is. Will it include weekend getaways, long vacations, cruises, or visits to family and friends? For short trips, you can build a monthly expense into your budget, putting the money you do not use into a pool for spending later. If you are planning for longer more expensive vacations, add a vacation fund to the budget. As we found out, this is one area retirees tend to under-budget and over-spend.

Clothing and personal care: How much do you spend to dress for work and spend on grooming? Will it be less in retirement?

Leisure Activities: Now that you may have more time in retirement, will you spend more on Entertainment such as movies, books, theater, or clubs? What about hobbies or recreational activities?

Pet Care: If you have pets, how much do you spend to feed and care for them?

Gifts and Charitable Giving: Many people forget to include money they use to buy gifts for family and friends or give to church or charities. Will this change once you retire?

Income Taxes: After you stop working you will be responsible for withholding taxes on income from taxable accounts and other sources of income from 401K or IRA accounts and capital gains from which you did not have income tax withheld. Some of your Social Security Benefits most likely will be taxed. You may be required to make estimated quarterly tax payments, so it is a good idea to review possible future tax implications that reduce spendable income. Appendix I can help you figure this out.

Health and medical expenses: Will you buy insurance to supplement Medicare gaps, or will you be paying for all your health care insurance until you are age 65 and become eligible for Medicare? Will you join a health club, or cancel a club membership?

Planning for health care costs can be especially daunting with estimated costs for an average 65-year-old couple retiring in 2019 hitting a total of $285,000 (in today's dollars) over their entire 30 year plus retirement period. Even if you are covered by Medicare and an insurance plan from your former employer, supplemental premiums and out-of-pocket costs continue to rise.

A study by Vanguard Research and Mercer Health and Benefits found that thirty-eight percent of baby boomers surveyed listed health care costs as their top fear about retirement, ahead of running out of money. Health care costs make up 9% to 14% of the average older household's spending. But what you will spend on health care costs in retirement could be less if you are generally healthy, or potentially a lot more if not in the best of health.

Trying to estimate what you will spend on future medical care may feel like an impossible exercise. But researchers have discovered that health care costs often fall into somewhat predictable patterns. In creating a model to help financial advisors predict clients' health care costs in retirement, Vanguard and Mercer assigned people to one of three risk categories:

- **Low risk** people do not smoke and generally are free of chronic health conditions.

- **Medium risk** people might smoke or visit the doctor more than a few times a year and have one or two chronic conditions.

- **High risk** people smoke or visit the doctor frequently or have two or more chronic conditions.

The researchers estimated health care costs for women, which are about 2% higher than those for men. Those at low risk could expect to pay roughly $3,000 to $4,300 per year. Those at medium risk $3,200 to $6,600 per year and those at high risk $3,500 to $21,000 per year. Also, a 65-year-old female could expect to spend about twice as much in real terms at age 85.

It is also likely that these healthcare costs will rise at about twice the rate of inflation or about 6% per year. As an example, that $350 per month cost at the beginning of retirement could become closer to $630 a month ten years later. For a married couple, you need to double these numbers.

However, the study also found that people who work past age 65 tend to be in better health and incur fewer medical expenses than those who retire earlier.

Covering Emergencies

Life has a way of throwing you curve balls that are unpredictable. Unexpected major expenses happen, so money should be set aside for these unplanned non-budgeted expenses. If your income sources are mostly guaranteed then the emergency fund only needs to cover the expense and not lost wages, so it can be lower than during your working years.

Since these events are unpredictable, it is not reasonable to include them in your budget. In chapter 4, Worksheet 3 will allow you to allocate money for an Emergency Fund, money you want to leave to your heirs or favorite causes, and any money you want to set aside to be used as a cushion for the later years of retirement or in case you or your spouse live longer than you were planning on. These amounts will then be subtracted from the total value of your savings and investments to arrive at the *spendable* portion, which is the amount you would like to spend during retirement. This amount will then be used in the appropriate Savings Withdrawals Worksheet in chapter 11 to determine the suggested safe annual withdrawal amount.

Budgeting Suggestions

The budgeting process usually stalls before it really gets started. Too often it is put off in hopes of getting to it later or because the focus is on the details of your discretionary (nice-to-have) spending which can be discouraging.

Focus on the big picture first. Start by understanding your ***essential expenses*** (must-haves) first. Health, comfort, and security are among life's most important priorities, so you will want to make health care, housing, transportation, and food your budget priorities. Once you have accounted for your "must-haves," you can begin budgeting your ***discretionary expenses*** (nice-to-have) by focusing on categories of spending like hobbies, dining out, gifting, entertainment and those bucket-list adventures you've been dreaming of.

You will need to get organized and plan-ahead. Think about the life you want to live in retirement. You need to know the details of your recent spending patterns, and determine whether your overall spending will go up, go down, or stay the same in retirement.

Tracking your spending has several benefits. First, it can give you a clear idea of exactly where your money is going each month. When you do not keep a close eye on your expenses, it is easy to overspend.

Another benefit of tracking your money is that it makes it easier to see if there are areas of your budget where you can cut back. Sometimes it is hard to see exactly how much you are spending on certain discretionary expenses, especially smaller costs like lunches and coffees that can really add up over a 12-

month period. Cutting just $10 per day adds up to $3,650 per year. When you have all your expenses laid out in front of you, it is easier to spot these trends and decide what discretionary expenses you can easily cut back on if needed.

Worksheet 1 at the end of this chapter, is a good checklist of items to include. Start by listing your average monthly recurring expenses like mortgage or rent, insurance, utility bills, telephone, and cable bills then determine how much money is coming in versus going out. Look at your bank statement year-end summaries to see where you spent the most money last year. Do the same with credit card statements.

Next, review your list of ongoing monthly bills and determine whether you need to continue all these services in retirement. Look through your past bills and bank statements to identify any work-related or other expenses that you may no longer have to pay when you retire. It is a great opportunity to think about which expenses will be important to your retirement enjoyment and which will not.

Your spending budget should be created at the beginning of each year. If you kept track of the previous year's spending it will be a big help in creating the current year budget. If you already have a spending budget system that you prefer to use, you can simply enter the total annual estimated spending amount in the appropriate Withdrawals Worksheet 4, 5, 6, or 7 that you will select in chapter 11.

As mentioned previously, it is especially important to separate your budget into *essential* needs or must-haves and *discretionary* wants or nice-to-have, to determine your **Budget Flexibility Percentage.** This becomes especially critical when the value of your investments suffer from an extended stock market downturn and you may need to reduce your discretionary spending.

At the bottom of worksheet 1 you will calculate the percent flexibility your budget has by dividing the total discretionary expenses by the total of all expenses. This flexibility percentage will be used in chapter 10 to help create upper and lower spending limit percentages that are designed to help smooth out year to year spending.

The goal is to create as realistic a spending budget as possible. Keeping track and recording what was spent each month helps you see where your money goes and how realistic your budget is. It also helps you see where you might be able to adjust your spending and helps improve accuracy over time. See Appendix II for a form to use to track annual expenses.

Keep in mind that you are creating a *desired* spending budget, and it may have to be adjusted later based on what the withdrawal system you select in chapter 11 *suggests* you can spend. It first determines the *safe* savings withdrawal amount and adds your expected after-tax income to arrive at the *suggested* spending budget.

Worksheet 1: Establishing your Desired Spending

Create at the beginning of each Year

Essential expenses:	ESTIMATED EXPENSES		ACTUAL EXPENSES	
	Monthly $	Annual $	Annual $	Over Budget
Housing:				
Mortgage or Rent				
Property taxes				
Homeowners insurance				
Utilities Water Gas Electric				
TV Phone & Internet				
Association Fees				
Maintenance/fees				
Other				
Food & Transportation:				
Groceries				
Auto Loan or lease payments				
Vehicle maintenance				
Fuel				
Auto insurance & Registration				
Public transportation				
Other				
Health care:				
Medical, Dental & Vision				
Medications and supplies				
Medicare/Medigap insurance				
Health insurance				
Other				
Personal insurance:				
Life insurance				
Disability insurance				
Long-term care insurance				
Other insurance				
Personal & Family care:				
Products and services				
Alimony Payment				
Child or Parent care				
Other				
Miscellaneous:				
Loans				
Pet Costs				
Banking & credit card fees				
Financial & Tax prep fees				
Other				
Total Essential expenses:				

Worksheet 1 continued

Discretionary expenses:	ESTIMATED EXPENSES		ACTUAL EXPENSES	
	Monthly $	Annual $	Annual $	Over Budget
Entertainment				
Clothing				
Dinning out				
Travel/vacation				
Hobbies				
Subscriptions				
Memberships				
Gifts				
Charitable contributions				
Education				
Other Discretionary				
Total Discretionary expenses:				

Total All expenses:			

Budget Flexibility %:
Divide Total Discretionary by Total all expenses

Note the "Monthly $" column is only used as a reference for those expenses that are close to the same every month but must also be annualized and entered into the "Annual $" column.

Chapter 3

Your Expected Income

In this chapter we will look at your potential sources of income and suggest ways to increase retirement income as well as sources of guaranteed income so that at least your essential fixed and non-discretionary expenses are covered.

Worksheet 2 at the end of the chapter is where you will identify your sources of retirement income. You will enter your estimated income for the current year, and at the beginning of each year in retirement. You will also need to estimate income taxes to determine your estimated after-tax spendable income. After you stop working you will be responsible for withholding taxes on income from taxable accounts and other sources of income including withdrawals from 401K or IRA accounts and capital gains if you did not withhold income tax. You may also have to pay income tax on part of your Social Security income depending on how much other income you receive.

You may be required to make quarterly tax payments, so it is a good idea to carefully review possible future tax implications that will reduce your spendable income. Appendix I Estimating Your Income Taxes provides some help, but you may need to consult with a Tax professional and or Financial Planner if you are not comfortable with these determinations.

Your retirement income plan should include *Guaranteed Income* such as Social security, Pensions, and possibly Annuities, to cover your fixed and essential non-discretionary expenses like food, housing, and health care. It also requires *Spending Flexibility* especially for your non-essential discretionary spending and to be able to refine your plan as needed over time.

When to take Social Security Benefits

Among the most critical retirement decisions you will have to make is when you and your spouse should start drawing Social Security. Even if you or your spouse are already drawing benefits, it is not too late to change your mind. Later in this chapter I show you how you can change your mind along with some additional reasons why you might want to do this.

Many financial planners recommend delaying receiving Social Security benefits until your 70th birthday. The reason is that for every year you postpone your benefits, they will be increased 8% until age 70. That is a 32% increase above your eligible benefit at 66 and 76% above you are benefit at 62. And remember that the increases are for the remainder of your life. Plus, the annual cost of living increases, are calculated as a percentage of the previous year's benefits, so the compounding effect of those increases over the length of your retirement can be large.

Some people think your full monthly benefit will be reinstated once you reach your full retirement age, but that's not how the program works which is why if you file at 62, the monthly benefit you lock in will generally be what you end up with for the rest of your life.

Social Security is technically designed to provide you with the same amount of lifetime income regardless of when you initially file. Though claiming benefits at 62 means slashing your monthly payments, you will collect a larger number of individual payments to offset that loss, thereby breaking even. However, this formula assumes that you will end up living an average lifespan. If your health or family history is good, you risk losing out on a lifetime of income by filing at 62 and the difference could be substantial.

A recent study by Massachusetts Mutual Life Insurance Company found that almost 40% of retirees regretted taking Social Security benefits early. They also found that even using the most conservative cumulative calculation, a married couple living into their early 90's could be forfeiting more than $500,000 or as much as $2000 to $4000 per month for life, by filing for Social Security benefits at age 62 versus age 70. The study also found that a surviving spouse could receive $1000 to $2000 per month less as a result of filing at 62.

Think of delaying social security as buying one of the best annuities plans you can get, paid for with the benefit money you would have received. As an example, delaying benefits four years, from age 66 to 70 years old, is like an annuity that pays for itself in about 13 to 16 years, or by the age of 83 to 86, based on the significant increase in benefit payments starting at age 70. In addition, the higher benefit amounts received beyond the break-even point will be at a time when they are often needed the most.

Note that the break-even point for recouping the value of delayed benefits is not a simple calculation since it is affected by inflation rates and by investment growth rates. Depending on if and how much of the early benefit payments are invested, or allows existing savings to not be spent, will allow the amount to grow longer. The lower the growth rate, the shorter the break-even period, because invested early withdrawals will grow slower. Also, the higher the inflation rate, the shorter the break-even period, because future higher benefit payments will compound faster with larger cost of living adjustments.

Of course, not everybody has the option to delay benefits until age 70. Many seniors are forced out of their jobs earlier in life, and when that happens, claiming benefits prior to or at full retirement age often becomes necessary.

While your situation may not appear to allow you to delay receiving benefits, depending on your income, and spending needs, it may make sense to tap other sources of income first such as:

- Some studies suggest that it may be advantageous for the lower earning spouse to take benefits early and the higher earning spouse to delay until age 70.

- Working part time at your old job, if that is a possibility, or other part-time work while in your 60s that pays an amount nearly equal to what your monthly benefit would have been if you took Social Security early might be a very good method to use.

- Maybe tap your savings that may only be earning 1-2% interest if you have more than what is needed to cover an emergency. But you should avoid selling investments that have growth potential.

- Depending on your income tax bracket it may make sense to withdraw from your 401K or IRA assuming you are older than 59.5 to avoid penalties.

If you use other sources to make up for delayed Social Security benefits, your goal should be to keep the withdrawals as low as possible.

Additional Reasons to Delay taking Social Security Benefits:

As I write this chapter, we are experiencing a major market crash, with countless seniors watching their retirement investments plummet in value as COVID-19 batters the U.S. economy and the stock market. While those that are many years from retirement may be well-positioned to wait out a downturn by leaving their savings alone, retirees who are already in the process of taking retirement plan withdrawals may not have that same option. Some retirees stand to take serious losses if they need to access money from their 401(k)s or IRAs soon.

That is where a higher Social Security benefit would have come in handy. The more money you collect in benefits each month, the less you will need to withdraw from your retirement savings to pay bills. The more you can leave your investments intact to grow and recover and avoid major losses, the more you will have to spend later in retirement.

Also, if you still plan to keep working, even part time, while drawing social security, you may have some benefits withheld. Though the Social Security Administration allows you to work and collect benefits simultaneously, if you do so prior to reaching your **Full Retirement Age** (known as FRA), you'll have a portion of your benefits withheld if your earnings exceed a certain threshold. In 2020, if you are below your full FRA, you will have $1 in Social Security withheld for every $2 you earn above $18,240. If you'll be reaching FRA at any point in 2020, you can earn up to $48,600 without impacting your benefits, but once you surpass that point, you'll have $1 in Social Security income withheld for every $3 you earn.

The amount of benefits Social Security withheld will be added back into your benefits once you reach FRA. But the reduction in basic monthly benefits you face by filing early will remain in effect on a permanent basis, which is why it often does not make sense to claim Social Security at 62 if you are still working.

When delaying does not make sense

Your health can play a major role in deciding when to take Social Security. If you have lived a healthy lifestyle and your family history has longevity you should wait. If you have health issues, waiting until age 70 does suggest you need to live to about 83 to break even.

If you die at an earlier age than the typical retiree, you will end up losing out on lifetime benefits by waiting, despite having secured a larger monthly benefit by delaying them.

The downside is if you guess wrong on how long you will live and you end up living past your breakeven age, you will have left money on the table and potentially a lot of money that may be needed near the end of an extended lifetime when you may need it the most.

You can change your mind

You can change your mind if you want larger monthly payments in the future. Once you claim your benefits Social Security gives you three options to change your mind:

- You can **Withdraw your application** for Social Security, but you have only 12 months to do this and you will have to return any amounts you received.

- You can **Suspend Benefits** after you reach your full retirement age.

- You can apply for a **Withdrawal of Benefits** prior to reaching your full retirement age. This is a formal process that, unlike a suspension, requires you to repay Social Security the benefits you have received to date.

If you can afford to do without your retirement benefit for a few years, it may make long-term financial sense to **Suspend Benefits**. During a **suspension**, you earn delayed retirement credits, which boost your eventual benefit by two-thirds of 1 percent for each suspended month (or 8 percent for each suspended year). When you resume collecting Social Security, you will have locked in a higher monthly payment for life.

You can ask Social Security to resume payments at any time until you turn 70. If you have not done it by then, Social Security will automatically reinstate your benefits in the higher amount.

As an example, say your full retirement age is 66 and you claimed benefits at 62. Filing early caused a monthly payment reduction of 25% compared with what you would have gotten if you had waited until age 66 to file. But if you suspend your benefits at age 66, you can qualify for an 8% boost to your monthly payment for each year you wait. The 8% is calculated based on that reduced payout, but if you suspend until age 70, you can get almost back to what you would have earned if you'd waited until full retirement age in the first place.

If for example your full retirement benefit would have been $2,400 per month but filing early reduced it to $1,800, suspending for four years will boost that $1,800 by 32%, or $576 per month. When you start taking payments again at age 70, you will get $2,376, adjusted for whatever is happened with inflation in the interim. That is almost back to the original $2,400 amount.

Another situation in which it can make sense to suspend your benefits is if your income from other sources rises unexpectedly, leaving you in a position in which a significant portion of your Social Security could be subject to income tax. If the sum of your outside income plus half your Social Security is greater than $25,000 for singles or $32,000 for joint filers, then you could end up having to include part of your Social Security benefits as taxable income for the year. Retirees can see fluctuations in income from part-time work, or from the taxable distributions they take from retirement accounts like 401(k)s or IRAs, or from capital gains.

Suspending benefits is only available after full retirement age, so a high-income year before that will leave you with no good alternatives. After that, though, it is worth considering if your tax planning indicates that you are likely to have higher than normal taxable income.

Keep in mind that for as long as your retirement benefits are suspended, your spouse and children cannot collect family benefits on your work record. Similarly, you cannot collect spousal benefits on your wife's or husband's record if your own retirement payments are suspended.

But if holding off on taking benefits is something you can do and is something that makes sense given your health and life expectancy, then it pays to consider boosting one of your most important retirement income streams for life. You never know when that higher monthly benefit will be needed and prevent you from taking significant financial losses that could affect the rest of your retirement years.

If all of this is confusing to you or you are still undecided on what to do, I highly recommend you seek the advice of a professional financial advisor or tax professional for help in making this critical decision.

The Income Tax Surprises!

Many retirees believe that their taxes will go down once they retire and will become simpler, but I have found the opposite to be true. The biggest surprise was the income tax on Social Security benefits, due to IRA withdrawals, Capital gains, and income from part time work that can easily increase income well above the threshold for taxes to be paid on benefits.

The tax is not easy to calculate, and is beyond the scope of this book, but as an example, for the 2019 tax year, a married couple filing jointly, will pay taxes on up to 50% of their Social Security income if their combined income is $32,000 to $44,000. If more than $44,000, they can expect to pay taxes on up to 85%. The IRS considers combined income as including one-half of your social security income, so it does not take much additional income before you start paying taxes on part of your social security income.

When we reached 70.5 years (before the change to age 72 in 2020) and had to start withdrawing the Required Minimum Distribution or RMD from our IRA's and pay taxes on it, we received a double surprise in that the amount of RMD withdrawn raised our combinable income level above the threshold for having 85% of our SSI benefits taxed.

Another surprise was having to file quarterly estimated income taxes, if you expect to owe more than $1000 above that which was paid through withholding. These complications, especially avoiding penalties, may require you to consult with a tax professional.

As you can see, it is important to estimate the amount of taxes you will pay in retirement so you can budget for it. In chapter 13 we will discuss ways to structure your retirement income so that you pay less taxes in retirement. In worksheet 2, you will need to estimate your annual after-tax income. In Appendix I: Estimating your Income Taxes, you will find additional help. If you are not comfortable with estimating your taxes you should seek help.

Should You Buy an Annuity?

As previously mentioned, your retirement income plan should include a source of **Guaranteed Income** such as Social security, Pensions, and possibly Annuities, to cover your fixed and essential non-discretionary expenses like food, housing, and health care. If all your essential living expenses will be covered by Social Security and a pension you probably do not need an annuity, especially if you are comfortable managing your investments. Also, if you are in poor health or not concerned with outliving your income and savings, you are probably not a good candidate for buying an annuity.

Annuities are offered by insurance companies and have had a bad reputation in the past for excessive fees, high sales commissions, high pressure sales techniques, and being sold with hard to understand fine print. However, because of more stringent government regulations put in place and reputable insurance companies simplifying the buying process, they can be a safe and valuable addition to your retirement income plan.

Annuities can solve the retirement spending dilemma by providing a guaranteed, lifetime income stream. While people with self-managed accounts worry about the retirement dilemma of spending a dollar today vs. saving that dollar for future expenses, those with an annuity can spend money today with the confidence that they can count on future income to meet expenses tomorrow. Annuities can also be valuable in getting retirees who are reluctant to spend, to spend money in retirement.

Purchasing an annuity may make sense if the following appeals to you:

- You are concerned about outliving your savings.

- You do not have enough guaranteed income to cover your essential living expenses.

- You want to know with little risk how much income you can count on for as long as you or your spouse lives.

- You have a lot of retirement savings but are not comfortable managing your own investments due to the risk and volatility involved.

- You do not want to pay someone to manage your money and want simple investments that do not require much attention.

One barrier to buying an annuity is the realization that you could die in the next few months or years, and not fully recover the amount spent for the annuity. On the other hand, you could live well beyond age 90, which means you could easily recoup more than the cost of the annuity.

This is just the nature of an income annuity. It is a bet on how long you will live. Die soon and you lose, live long and you win. But which is the worse outcome, being alive and broke in your 90's or regret from the grave that you died too soon to recoup your investment? I will take the latter.

There are basically two types of annuities, **Immediate Annuities** and **Deferred Annuities.** With immediate annuities you hand over a considerable amount of cash to the insurance company and in exchange the company starts giving you monthly payments of an agreed-upon amount. An immediate annuity can be a great choice for a new retiree with lots of retirement savings who is not comfortable managing his own investments. By handing over a large chunk of that retirement savings for an annuity contract, you are putting the responsibility on the insurance company for making that money work. And regardless of how the company's investments perform, it is still required to pay you the amount specified in the contract.

Unlike immediate annuities, deferred annuities allow you to put money down in advance of when you want to receive payments. You can invest in a deferred annuity long before you hit retirement age. After you hand over your money to the insurance company, it will sit in your account and accrue returns based on the terms of your annuity contract. The longer you leave your investment alone, the more it is likely to grow.

Deferred annuities typically give you several options for getting your money, including lump-sum where you get your entire payment at once, systematic withdrawal where you periodically withdraw funds until your account is empty, and annuitization where you lock in a regular schedule of payments for a certain length of time including lifetime.

As long as you haven't annuitized your deferred annuity, you'll have access to the money you've contributed and can withdraw part of it or all of it if you cancel the contract, but you may have to pay surrender fees. Once you annuitize, you will be locked into the payments set by your contract and will no longer be able to withdraw the money you have invested.

I would advise against purchasing *variable annuities* or *equity-indexed annuities* which typically have higher costs and the amount of money you receive is somewhat tied to how the stock market or other underlying investment will perform in the future. The variability in payouts may not meet a retiree's need to have a fixed and known income that can be counted on for the remainder of their life.

A **Qualified Longevity Annuity Contract (QLAC)** is a special type of annuity created in 2014 when the US Treasury Department issued a rule creating QLACs. If you have a traditional IRA or 401(k), you must begin taking mandatory minimum yearly withdrawals, known as Required Minimum Distributions or RMDs from these accounts when you reach 72. (The rules regarding the age you must start taking the RMD changed with the passing of the SECURE Act which became law on December 20, 2019).

But what if you do not need the money from your IRA RMD for current living expenses and would prefer to receive guaranteed lifetime income later in retirement? QLACs allow you to use a portion of your balance in qualified accounts like a traditional IRA or 401(k) to purchase a deferred income annuity and not have that money be subject to RMDs starting at age 72.

A QLAC is a deferred income annuity that can be funded only with money from a traditional IRA or a 401(k), 403(b), or governmental 457(b). At the time of purchase, you can select an income start date up to age 85, and the amount you invest in a QLAC is removed from future RMD calculations.

There are rules, however, about how much money you can use to fund a QLAC. There are two limitations: Total lifetime contributions cannot exceed $135,000 across all funding sources, and QLAC contributions from a given funding source cannot exceed 25% of that funding source's value.

According to the 2019 Retirement Confidence Survey conducted by the Employee Benefit Research Institute, more than 30% of American workers were not confident they will have enough money to maintain their standard of living throughout their retirement. A QLAC may be a good option.

A QLAC delivers a guaranteed stream of lifetime income beginning on the date you choose. For example, you might purchase a QLAC at age 66 and have your payouts begin at age 75. Typically, the longer the deferral period, the higher your payout will be when you are ready to start receiving income payments.

When do you want income to start?

Deciding on when to purchase an annuity income start date will depend on how the income payments will best fit into your retirement plan. Here are some hypothetical examples of how you might choose an income start date:

- A 65-year-old retiree with an existing income stream that will become much lower at age 75 because of say a planned sale of a business or sale of a rental property might want the annuity to start paying income at age 76 to replace the income that is ending.

- A couple in their late 60s might like to include an income stream that begins at age 80 or 85 as part of their retirement plan, to help cover higher expected health costs later in retirement.

- A couple at age 65 might be comfortable taking withdrawals from their savings and investments to cover their expenses at the beginning of their retirement, but they are concerned about the potential need for it to last 30 years or more. They might consider an annuity that provides lifetime income starting at age 80, to eliminate the risk of outliving their savings.

Should you wait until at least age 80 to buy an Annuity?

A growing number of advisors including Bogleheads.org make a very good case of waiting until at least age 80 to buy an *inflation-indexed* Single Premium Immediate Annuity (SPIA), so that total *non-savings* income (including Social Security, pension, and other lifelong income) is sufficient to live comfortably and independently of future savings withdrawals. The main purpose is to reduce the financial and longevity risks associated with living past age 95.

It is important to consider using only part of your remaining savings to buy a SPIA, and to buy only as much as you need. Remember that a SPIA represents an irrevocable commitment of your savings required to purchase it, and the resultant loss of control over them. It should only be used to fill a gap between your other sources of guaranteed income and your expected minimum monthly spending needs over the course of your lifetime. Preferably less than 50% of your savings value should be spent purchasing a SPIA.

By waiting until age 80, SPIA's payout significantly more per month than if you bought one at say 70 for the same initial cost. As a recent example, buying a SPIA with $100,000 paid upfront that covers only your life, will provide approximately $560 per month if purchased at age 70 which equals an annual average return of 6.7%. If you wait until age 80 it will pay approximately $880 per month which equals an annual average return of 10.6%. If you want it to cover both you and your spouse, the payment drops roughly 20% since it will have to continue making payments to whichever one lives longer. See Appendix IV References & Resources, Chapter 3 for a reference to this important topic.

How risky are annuities? Whenever you go shopping for an annuity you must consider the financial strength of the insurance company you purchase from. Annuities are guarantees to provide you specific income amounts, and those guarantees are only as good as the company behind those guarantees. It is preferable to stick with an "A" rated company and one of the most common rating scales for annuities is A.M. Best. On their website you can see their rating scale.

Buying an annuity that you expect to receive income from for 15 or more years is a long time, and a lot can happen over that period. Insurance companies are backed by "state guaranty associations." These associations help pay for claims if your annuity company goes bankrupt. Not all annuities are covered under the state guaranty associations. Each state guaranty association has different levels of protection. No state offers less than $100,000 in annuity protection. And some states, like New York, offer up to $500,000.

If you decide an annuity meets your needs, make sure to check the annuity contract for any surprises. Make sure you thoroughly understand all the fees involved with the contract and compare them with one or two other, similar annuity contracts to confirm that they are not excessive.

Navigating the complexities of annuities is not easy and the financial consequences can have major implications. Consulting with a financial advisor who can explain each option, and how it fits into your overall retirement plan can reduce a lot of the anxiety and complexity.

Worksheet 2: Expected Annual After-Tax Income

Create at the beginning of each Year

	Current Year Income		
	You	Your Partner	
Social Security:			
Pensions:			
Annuities:			
Employment Income:			
Rental Income:			
Dividend & Interest #1:			(Note 1 below)
Dividend & Interest #2:			
Other Income #1:			
Other Income #2:			
Other Income #3:			
Total Annual Income:			
Less Federal Income Tax:			(Note 2 below)
Less State Income Tax:			
Less Other Taxes:			
Total Annual After Tax Income:			(See Note 3 below)

Notes:

(1) Do not include any Dividends that are reinvested in stocks or bonds

(2) It should be noted that any income taxes that you may owe due to withdrawing from your investments including IRA RMD's should be estimated and entered into this section. Enter as Negative Numbers

(3) Combine amounts & enter total in the appropriate Withdrawal Worksheet. If you have your own estimated annual income system just enter the amount in the Withdrawal Worksheet instead of using this expected income sheet. Make sure the amount is the Annual After-Tax Income.

Chapter 4

Do You Have Enough Saved?

We will attempt to answer this important question but first you need to know what you currently have saved for retirement. Worksheet 3, at the end of this chapter, should be used to estimate the total savings & investments available to be withdrawn and used specifically to support your desired lifestyle over the length of your retirement.

The worksheet will allow you to allocate money for the following:

- **Emergency Funds** - Unexpected major expenses happen, so money should be set aside for these unplanned non budgeted expenses. If your income sources are mostly guaranteed, then the emergency fund only needs to cover the expense and not lost wages so it can be much lower than during your working years.

- **Bequeaths to Heirs** – The amount you want to leave to your heirs or to your favorite causes.

- **Money Cushion** – An Optional amount of money to hedge against living longer than planned or to provide for additional health expenses in the later years of retirement.

- **Reserve fund** – An Option you can use to smooth year to year spending variability caused by how well your investments performed the previous year. It is used instead of setting spending limits as discussed in Chapter 10.

These amounts are subtracted from the total to determine the *Spendable* portion of your Savings & Investments that you plan to use to help fund your retirement. This amount is used in chapter 11 in the appropriate Withdrawals Worksheet to arrive at the suggested safe withdrawal and safe spending amounts.

Note that I may interchangeably use the terms Savings, Investments, Portfolio, or Portfolio Value throughout the remainder of the book to mean basically the same thing.

Your Retirement Number

You may or may not have determined what a lot of advisor's call, your *Retirement Number*, which is the amount of savings you think you need to have accumulated before you can afford to retire.

Here is a rough calculation that can determine your Retirement Number to see how close you are to having enough to retire. Either take your last 12 months of spending or preferably your desired annual spending from Worksheet 1, then subtract your expected annual after-tax income preferably from Worksheet 2. This will determine the approximate annual shortfall needed to be covered by your savings, then multiply the annual shortfall by 25. If your savings and investments determined in Worksheet 3, are close to or exceed this number, your retirement is close at hand. If not, you may need to reduce spending, delay retirement, or both.

The multiplier of 25 is based on the 4% rule as detailed in chapters 8 and 9. The 4% rule is based on a famous study that indicated you could safely withdraw 4% of your savings each year at the start of a 30 year or longer retirement without outliving your retirement savings. Although it has fallen out of favor with many financial planners it is still useful as a rough estimate of the savings needed to fund your retirement.

As an example, if you plan to live on $5,500 a month in retirement and expect $2500 a month in Social Security benefits and $1000 per month from a pension, your monthly shortfall will be $2000 per month or $24,000 per year. Multiply this by 25 to arrive at your **retirement number** of $600,000 which is the amount you should have in savings and investments to fund your retirement.

A much more accurate determination of how much you can really safely withdraw and what you can afford to safely spend each year without outliving your savings will be made in chapter 11, but first we will review opportunities for you to consider that could make a significant difference in your retirement.

Should You Work Longer?

If you are satisfied with your *retirement number* and feel you have the resources to retire when you want to, you can ignore this section. However, the single most effective way to improve your retirement number and maintain or improve your standard of living once you retire, is to delay retirement, for as long as you can, or at least work part time.

A report from the Stanford Center on Longevity and Society of Actuaries that the typical American would benefit significantly by delaying even just a couple of years. The study showed that for a typical 62-year-old middle income couple, delaying retirement from 62 to 66 would increase the amount they could safely spend in retirement by $15,500 per year for the rest of their lives.

Maybe you have already determined that you will have to or will want to work longer than originally planned. The following summarizes the major benefits of delaying retirement:

- If you are still working, you do not have to draw down your savings to cover expenses and you can use part of your income to add to savings thus improving your retirement number.

- Working longer also allows existing investments to grow more especially if markets are performing well.

- If you are near retirement and your investments are performing poorly due to a market downturn, delaying drawing down your investments by working allows time for your investments to recover.

- Using the income from working longer between the ages of 62 and 70, can allow you to delay taking Social Security benefits thus greatly increasing your monthly benefit for the rest of your life.

- The Social Security Administration uses an average of your 35 highest years of earnings to determine your benefit amount so if you worked more than 35 years your lowest earning years are replaced with your higher earning years after being adjusted for inflation. By working longer, if your current earnings replace a lower earning year, your benefits will be recalculated higher. Even if your current wage is less than previous years, Social Security will still compute your benefits based on your highest 35 years.

- Working longer reduces the length of time you will need your savings to last thus increasing the amount you can withdraw each year. Chapter 11 looks at the impact that the age you start retirement and the length you want your savings to last will have on your safe withdrawal amounts.

- If you are younger than 65 the age when Medicare kicks in, by continuing your employment if possible, may allow you to take advantage of healthcare and other employer benefits.

Worksheet 3: Total Spendable Value of Your Portfolio

Total Portfolio amount available to be spent during retirement Create at the beginning of each Year		
	Value End of Previous Year	**See Notes below**
Savings #1:		
Savings #2:		
Savings #3:		
Investment #1:		If you have more savings & Investment Accounts Than Listed combine accounts
Investment #2:		
Investment #3:		
Investment #4:		
Investment #5:		
Investment #6:		
Roth IRA #1		
Roth IRA #2		
IRA or 401K #1:		
IRA or 401K #2:		
IRA or 401K #3:		
Savings & Investment Total:		
Credit Card Balances:		
Emergency Fund:		
Bequeaths to Heirs:		
Cushion if you live longer than planned		
Optional Reserve Fund:		
Total Reductions:		

Total Portfolio amount available to spend in retirement:		Subtract Total reductions from Savings & Investment total

Notes:
(1) Do not include the value of Annuities, Life Insurance, Home, Auto or other personal items.
(2) Enter the Total Portfolio amount available to be spent in retirement in the appropriate Withdrawal System Worksheet that is selected.

Chapter 5

Test Drive Your Retirement Decisions

You typically have only one shot at retiring correctly, So, don't jump into the many decisions you will have to make prior to retiring, too quickly. You would not think to buy a new car without taking it for a test drive so why would you not **Test Drive** your retirement decisions before you implement them?

Practicing retirement is a way to dip your toe in the retirement waters before diving in. Are you really ready financially and emotionally? Where are the holes or gaps in your plan? What decisions would be difficult to undo after you make them? Practicing retirement allows for you to make some mistakes and experience things you might find are not what you thought or better than you thought.

The idea of test-driving retirement, whether by cutting expenses, staying for a few weeks at a potential retirement destination, or staying at home for a week without work, makes sense but is harder than you might think. You might start out by first taking a one-week vacation and staying home. You really need to slow down first and set your expectations properly to make the test-drive valuable.

So, what does a retirement test drive look like? Much of that answer will depend on your needs, wants and goals, but the following ideas may help you in creating your own test-drive:

- Live on the income you expect to have in retirement. Try spending like a retired person. Ideally, you should try living your retirement lifestyle within your anticipated retirement budget for a full month to the best of your ability. Make a list of what you learned each day during the test-drive. Are you spending more than you anticipated? If you cannot live according to your retirement budget while you are still working, there is a good chance you will not be able to when you have lots of time on your hands to spend money.

- If you think you might want to move after you retire, look at spending as much time as you can at the new location to make sure it offers the benefits you are expecting. You need to understand what it is really like to live there. Experience the weather, the lifestyle, the access to entertainment, and good medical care. Determine what costs might change if you were to move there.

- Even with lots of travel plans, you most likely will spend a lot of your time at home after you retire. What will you spend this time on? Start by listing the things you want to do or make happen each week. It could be a good time to check out some of your interests (hobbies, passions, priorities) to better prepare to follow them in retirement.

- If you have a partner, this test-drive is an ideal time to get used to the idea that once you are both retired, you will be spending a lot more together. That can be a real challenge for even the most together relationships. During the COVID-19 pandemic when families were forced to shelter in place and spend 24/7 together, divorce and domestic abuse incidents increased significantly. Set aside time each week to do some things together, as well as time to pursue each of your own interests.

- In the pursuit of a healthier lifestyle or living longer, taking time for regular physical activity is important. Test-driving some new healthy additions or changes could be the beginning of a health regime that continues well into to retirement.

During your test-drive, you may discover that your travel, entertainment, or home maintenance costs are higher or lower than expected, that you want to live more simply than you had anticipated, or that you really do need more money to live the retirement lifestyle you want.

Test-driving your retirement might reveal some personal surprises. One spouse may find they are tired of working and are ready to retire, while the other spouse may find they are not. Is your spouse or partner in agreement with your conclusions? If not, what may need to change? Talking openly about each of your desires may reveal some surprises in terms of finances, timing, and lifestyle. Finding ways to fill your days with whatever it is that makes you both happy is no easy task.

There are obviously limitations to the test drive approach. It is a short-term experiment, but you need to resist taking shortcuts and not spending enough time seriously test driving your important decisions. I would recommend writing down all the important retirement decisions you will be making and prioritizing them with those that would be most difficult to undo in retirement listed first and at least test drive those.

Chapter 6

Navigating the Risks to your Retirement Plan

You can plan for your retirement and work to create the lifestyle you envision but there are no guarantees in life that you will achieve it. However, there are some risks that even if unknown, can be dealt with in your retirement planning. There are four major risks that cannot be known:

- **Longevity risk** is not knowing how long you or your spouse will live.

- **Market risk** is the possibility that poor market returns will significantly reduce or deplete your spendable investments too soon and thus produce a less than desirable retirement.

- **Inflation risk** is not knowing how much your spending will rise or how much your savings will be eroded later in retirement.

- **Unexpected spending risk** or major unplanned expenses such as major health expenses or helping a child or parents, that can reduce the available savings that were being counted on for an enjoyable retirement.

There are three basic ways to deal with risk: ***avoid it, manage it, or transfer it***. We face risks every day. You could have a serious accident while driving to work. You could *avoid it* by working from home, you could *manage* it by wearing a seat belt and driving defensively. Or, you could *transfer* it by taking the bus.

It's the same with financial risks, like the risk of loss you take when you invest, or the risk that inflation will erode the future value of your savings, or that you may run out of money in retirement. Some of these risks you can avoid, others you need to manage, and some you can transfer. Each method has its advantages and disadvantages. Understanding this can help you make better money decisions. Chapter 14 Investing for Growth will address investment risk in much more detail.

The Risk of long-term care

Although 48% of retirees will not incur long term care costs, for those who do, it can get expensive, fast. Temporary care (for example, to recover from a surgery or an accident) falls under Medicare Part A, so it would be at least partially covered. But Medicare does not cover ongoing long-term care.

A recent study found that of those needing long term care, 25% will incur expenses up to $100,000, 11% will incur between $100,000 to $250,000, and 16%

will be faced with more than $250,000 in long term care costs.

Long-term care includes anything from adult day care to residence at an assisted living facility to nursing care. Unless you have long-term care insurance, you will likely pay these costs out of pocket. And even insurance will typically start paying only after a predetermined period, and then only pay up to certain limits. If you exhaust all your financial resources, Medicaid may pay these types of costs.

The Greatest Risk to your Retirement Plan

I believe the greatest threat to achieving and maintaining the retirement lifestyle you want is that of your investments performing poorly for an extended period just before or in the early years of your retirement. This threat is known as the **"sequence of returns"** risk. This risk may significantly reduce the income available during retirement.

The potential impact is that you either outlive your savings or are forced to significantly reduce your spending, especially in your latter years when you may need it the most. Think 2008 when the market lost almost half its value, and although it more than recovered over the next 10 years, it was devastating to those that retired then.

Two retirees starting with the exact same investment amounts can have entirely different financial results, depending on how the economy is performing near the start of their retirement, even if the long-term market averages are the same. For example, a person entering retirement near the beginning of a bear market will see a reduction in the overall return of their investments because of how much had to be withdrawn early in retirement when values were down. Also, this retiree must withdraw funds as his or her investments are losing value. Consequently, with less equities this retiree will not be able to benefit as much when the market recovers.

By contrast, someone who retires near the beginning of a bull market when stock prices are rising, lets this investor take early withdrawals of higher value investments, because they are rising in value and most likely will have a higher overall investment return than the bear market retiree earns. The reason is the bull market retiree has more equities remaining which can allow this retiree to benefit from continued strong market returns later in retirement.

What many retirees do not consider is the sequence in which these returns occur. Even though the market has returned 7 to 9% per year on average and may continue to average this over the next 30 years, there is no way you will know which years and for how many years the market will be up and which years it will be down.

Therefore, I believe one of the biggest risks to your retirement is not the risk that the markets will go down significantly as they will do from time to time. The real risk is that the very worst returns occur in the early years of your retirement.

However, Investors have some options to better protect their investments against this risk, including the following:

- Having a cash cushion that can cover several years of expenses will lessen the need to significantly reduce spending or reduce the need to sell more risky investments when the values are down. Many financial advisors recommend having two to three years' worth of cash to be able to reduce the sequence of returns risk.

- Delay retirement and the need to make withdrawals until the market's performance improves. Not only will this allow you to leave your investments untapped for a longer period, but it will give you a chance to increase your savings. It might also allow you to delay Social Security and raise your benefits. Continuing to make contributions to retirement funds will allow you to buy at lower prices during the market downturn and provide for investments to continue to grow.

- A part-time job is a good way to supplement your income to reduce the need for larger savings withdrawals and buy time for your investments to grow, providing more options later in life. It is also an inexpensive way to occupy your newfound free time.

- Use a savings withdrawal system such as the 1/N, RMD, or VPW withdrawal system discussed in chapters 8 & 9. The amount you can withdraw is based on a specified percentage of the previous year's savings and investment balance. This may be painful, requiring significant reductions in spending by delaying all discretionary expenses and implementing cost cutting measures until your investments recover. Having a very flexible spending budget by keeping fixed and essential costs low will make this less painful.

On a personal note, in 2006 we decided we would like to retire at the end of 2010 at the age of 66 but delay taking Social Security until age 70. I was fortunate to have a job I still enjoyed and that allowed me to decide when I was ready to retire.

When the great recession hit two years later in 2008 our investments fell close to 30%, We decided to delay our retirement plans and continue to work to prevent having to sell and withdraw any investments that were now undervalued. This provided more time for our investments to grow and recover.

Continuing to work also allowed me to keep contributing to my Roth IRA and 401K, as well as receive employer contributions, all of which helped to accelerate investment growth. The hope was that we could still reach our Retirement Number that would allow achieving the retirement lifestyle we envisioned.

Eventually stock prices began rising to the point that our portfolio had recovered the entire drop in value within 2 years. This allowed me to ease into retirement by reducing my workload gradually, until the end of 2015 when I fully retired.

Chapter 7

Will you need a Financial Advisor or Planner?

Creating your retirement plan including the creation of an income, spending, and investing plan along with managing risks takes knowledge, skill, effort, discipline, and time which may be more than you feel comfortable doing or want to deal with.

Remember you are retiring to do the things you never had time for when you were working. Even if you are a do-it-yourselfer, there are lots of resources to help you to simplify or fill in any gaps in your retirement plan. Depending on how complex your situation is, you may want to consider working with a Financial Planner, a Financial Advisor or both. The following are some reasons you may want to consider getting professional advice:

- You and your partner may have different views regarding how much you can spend or how much risk to take investing and need an objective outside voice to help resolve differences.

- You need help creating a retirement investment plan that you can be comfortable with.

- You have difficulty developing detailed plans or sticking to a plan.

- You just need some occasional help to review your retirement plan and help you stay on track.

- A major life event happens like receiving an inheritance or going through a divorce or other financial event that might require help in dealing with it.

There are several varieties of financial advisors, including online robo-advisors, online financial planning services, and traditional face-to-face financial advisors.

Robo-advisors

Robo-advisors are computer-based services that help you choose and manage investments. They are a great, low-cost fit if interested specifically in investment management. A robo-advisor will build and manage an investment portfolio for you based on your goals, time frame and risk tolerance. Robo-advisors often require no or a low account minimum, so it is an easy way for those with lower account balances to get investing help.

Online financial planning services

These services operate online like robo-advisors but function more like traditional financial advisors. They may offer full-service, customized financial planning alongside investment management. Unlike with a traditional financial advisor with face to face planning, planning is done through phone or video meetings. Account minimums range from zero to a few hundred thousand dollars.

The way online financial planning services work varies. Some are robo-advisors with an added human element, offering computer-managed investments and access to a team of financial advisors for planning guidance and advice. Others offer each client a dedicated certified financial planner who works with you to build your investment portfolio and create a complete financial plan. In general, online financial planning services cost more than robo-advisors but less than a traditional in-person financial advisor.

Traditional face-to-face financial advisors

This is what most people think of when they think of a financial advisor, where you go to meet with your advisor in person at their office. Not every financial advisor is a financial planner, but every financial planner is a type of financial advisor. The National Association of Personal Financial Advisors NAPFA, claims there are more than 100 certifications available that a financial advisor might obtain.

A *Financial Planner* is a professional who helps companies and individuals create a plan to meet long-term financial goals. They might have a specialty in retirement planning, investments, taxes, and/or estate planning. Further, they may hold various licenses or designations, such as Certified Financial Planner (CFP), Chartered Financial Analyst (CFA), Chartered Financial Consultant (ChFC), or Certified Investment Management Analyst (CIMA), among others. To obtain each of these designations, the financial planner must complete a different set of education, examination, and work history requirements.

A *Financial Advisor* is a professional who helps you manage your money. You pay the advisor, and in exchange, they help with any number of money-related tasks. A financial advisor might help manage investments, broker the sale and purchase of stocks, bonds, and mutual funds, or create a comprehensive estate and tax plan. The advisor should hold a Series 65 license as well as other financial credentials, depending upon the services they provide.

Many planners and advisors may do the same thing, so do your homework before hiring somebody to assist and guide you. According to the Financial Industry Regulatory Authority (FINRA), almost anyone can claim to be a financial advisor and might come from many different backgrounds. A financial advisor might be a financial planner, investment adviser or stockbroker, insurance agent, accountant, money manager, or estate planner. They may not have any financial credentials at all. You must be careful and perform due diligence before turning your hard-earned money over to any type of financial advisor.

What to look for

Most individuals who will need help in creating a well thought out retirement plan will enlist the help of a face-to-face financial planner. Those with substantial investments may also need a financial advisor. ***Do not hire anyone that is going to give you financial advice and possibly manage your money without conducting due diligence, including those recommended by friends or relatives.*** So, what should you look for in choosing an advisor? The following list should help:

1. Hire an Advisor Who Is a Fiduciary. By definition, a fiduciary is an individual who is ethically bound to act in another person's best interest. This obligation eliminates conflict of interest concerns and makes an advisor's advice more trustworthy.

2. You should take your time to interview at least a few advisors before picking the best match for your needs. Consider developing a list of questions to ask during the interview.

3. Choose an advisor with the right specialty. Some advisors specialize in retirement planning, while others are best for business owners or those with a high net worth. Some might be best for young

professionals starting a family. Make sure you understand an advisor's strengths and weaknesses.

4. Ask your advisor about their licenses, tests, and credentials. If you need help with building a financial plan make sure they are a Certified Financial Planner, or CFP. In order to earn the CFP® mark you have to complete an approved financial planning curriculum, pass an exam, work as a financial planner for a certain number of years, adhere to an ethics code, and complete ongoing continuing education. You can verify their claim to be a CFP at www.cfp.net

5. An advisor might appear qualified and professional due to an association with a major investment firm. Working with an advisor from a reputable firm may or may provide any advantages, so make sure you choose an advisor because they are the best fit, not because of their affiliations.

6. Some advisors are "fee only" and charge you a flat rate no matter what. Others charge a percentage of your assets under management. Some advisors receive commissions from products they sell which could be a serious conflict of interest.

7. Do not be afraid to ask for references of current clients whose goals and finances match yours. This will give you a good idea as to the advisor's ability to help meet your requirements or not.

8. Run a background check on your planner. Start by asking: Have you ever been convicted of a crime? Have you ever been under investigation by any regulatory body or industry group?

How to Measure your Financial *Advisor's* Performance

You need to be cautious of any investment professional who promises you above-average account performance or says you will be making risk-free investments. Nobody can guarantee that your investments will grow at a certain rate or that you will not lose money.

Unfortunately, many brokers and advisors simply do not beat market returns. Some research suggests that returns from advisor-assisted accounts lag the results from those who handle their accounts on their own. Even when adjusting for the riskiness of the investments the advisor-led accounts still notably underperformed self-managed accounts. Brokers and advisors tend to use mutual funds, and research has shown that roughly three-quarters of mutual funds fail to beat their benchmarks.

It is also worth noting, that successful investment returns do not always mean beating a specific benchmark. It is about knowing the client's goals and getting the returns necessary to meet those goals. You need to be careful when talking about investment returns without considering the risk you are taking to earn those returns.

In a perfect world, financial advisors would tell you exactly how they should be measured, and some do. You should keep a report card and be ready to discuss his or her grades and what needs to change or improve.

The following are some key questions you should be asking, preferably after the year is over, regarding the investment performance your advisor achieved:

- Are my investment returns clearly displayed and easy to understand?

- Are my returns compared to applicable benchmarks?

- Are my returns beating their benchmarks?

- Is my broker or advisor willing to walk me through any aspect of the performance that I have difficulty understanding?

How to Measure your Financial Planner's Performance

Why did you select this Planner in the first place? Is he or she guiding you in the direction you intended or not? In my view, a financial planner should be evaluated at two stages, During the *Financial Plan Creation* stage and during the *Post Plan* stage.

During the **Financial plan Creation** stage, you need to evaluate the quality of discussions you are having with your financial planner. Are they going as you had hoped? Is your planner following a well thought out process? Does he or she discuss your financial data, goals, and your requirements? How will they decide on a suitable asset allocation for you and have they explained the risks involved? What are their views on your insurance coverage and your tax situation?

You need to be comfortable with your planner and should not be pressured or sold products in the name of planning. You need to be honest and if uncomfortable, it is better to immediately discuss this and if needed find another planner.

The **Post plan evaluation stage** is where the planner's role takes on more significance. It will take some time to judge the success of your financial plan in achieving your long and short-term goals, which may take several years to reach.

You cannot evaluate everything on numbers alone, especially financial planning, by just looking at investment returns. There are many aspects which generally do not get measured, like adjusting asset allocation to suit your risk tolerance, how your debt is handled, getting out of unsuitable insurance policies, and estate planning advice to name a few.

You should not ignore Investment Returns completely. But how much is the expectation and what should be reasonably assumed, should be decided during this stage. Any review of actual financial performance in relation to the financial plan, should include a comparison to appropriate benchmarks.

Advisor Fees

Many people think working with a financial advisor is out of their budget. That may have been true several years ago, but affordable financial advice is increasingly available. How much a financial advisor costs will depend on what kind of guidance you need and the type of advisor you choose.

Robo-advisor costs

Robo-advisors typically charge a fee of 0.25% to 0.50% of assets under management (AUM) which works out to $250 to $500 a year on a $100,000 account balance. Portfolios are created and monitored using computer algorithms. Robo-advisors generally do not provide customized financial plans or personalized investment advice, but many do offer online planning tools and calculators.

Online financial planning services costs

Online planning services charge either an AUM fee that ranges from 0.30% to 0.90%, or a flat annual fee that starts at about $400 a year and can go up to as much as several thousand dollars, depending on the level of financial advice you need. Note that some services might charge for investment management and financial planning separately. You will receive investment management, a comprehensive financial plan and ongoing access to financial planners for less than the cost of a traditional face-to-face advisor. Many services provide each client a dedicated CFP and meetings are usually held by phone or video.

Traditional face-to-face financial advisor costs

Traditional face-to-face advisors use a variety of fee structures. Some advisors do not think the fee they would collect on a small balance is worth their time and will not take on clients with less than $250,000 to $500,000. The following are some of the most common fees and typically what you get for that fee:

Assets Under Management (AUM) Fee: This is like what robo-advisors and many online planning services use. The median AUM fee among human advisors is about 1% of assets managed per year, with some starting higher for small accounts and becoming less as your balance increases. You should receive investment management, and in some cases, a comprehensive financial plan and guidance for how to achieve that plan. However, some advisors who charge an AUM fee offer only investment management, not planning services. You will typically have an ongoing relationship with the advisor.

Retainer for Services: A set monthly or annual fee. The cost usually is not linked to how much you have available to invest, but you may pay more if your situation is complicated. Cost ranges from $2,000 to $7,500 a year. You should receive comprehensive planning and investment management. The advisor will create a financial plan, help you implement it, monitor your progress, and adjust as needed.

Hourly Rate: Some financial planners have a set hourly rate, which does not change based on your AUM. You only pay for the time you need. Cost is typically $200 to $400 an hour. You can schedule a few meetings to check your retirement savings progress, receive help with budgeting, or if you want a full financial plan. You carry out the plan on your own and there is no ongoing oversight unless you request and pay for additional time.

Flat Fee per Plan: Some advisors charge a flat fee for creating a financial plan. There is no ongoing management or oversight and you execute the plan yourself. The cost will vary by service, but $1,000 to $3,000 is typical for a financial plan. You should receive a comprehensive financial plan and guidance for how to follow it, but no ongoing services or investment management. The advisor charges a set fee for each type of service. You should get an outline of what is included for the fee.

Pay Attention to how Fees are structured

A Fee-only advisor does not earn any commissions from the services provided. These advisors face the fewest conflicts of interest when offering advice. They may combine more than one fee type such as charging a flat fee for financial planning and an AUM fee for investment management.

A Commission-only advisor receives their income from commissions on the investments bought and sold on your behalf. I do not recommend using commission-based financial advisors due to conflict of interest issues. While some put your needs first, others may be influenced by the product that pays the highest commission. The advisor may only be required to recommend investments that are suitable for you but may not necessarily be the best fit.

A financial advisor can be a great asset when it comes to helping you with your retirement planning. No matter which type of financial service you choose, be sure to understand exactly how much you will be paying for the services rendered and what you expect to receive from those services. You need to be careful because the fees can add up quickly.

Chapter 8

A Better System of Spending Your Savings

The goal is to make your savings last as long as you do so that you can continue to live comfortably in the latter years of retirement. There are many retirement savings withdrawal systems that have been created and studied over the years. They are all designed to make your savings last as-long-as you do while attempting to manage the risks of failure.

After having studied many different withdrawal systems, I chose what I believe are the four most often recommended and thoroughly tested savings withdrawal systems in use today. They each have advantages and disadvantages and are impacted differently by the amount of investment gains, inflation rates, and your allocation of Stocks to Bonds to Cash. The impact of these variables is discussed in more detail in this chapter and the following chapter. For a reference to the historical financial performance over the last 90 years see Appendix III Table 5A.

The four withdrawal systems chosen for consideration are the 4% Withdrawal system, the 1/N Withdrawal system, the IRS Required Minimum Distribution (RMD) Withdrawal system, and the Variable Percentage Withdrawal (VPW) system. This book will guide you in choosing which of the four withdrawal systems you are most comfortable with.

Left out of this book is the withdrawal strategy that suggest you only spend the interest and dividends your investments generate each year and not touch the principal. Very few of us have the wealth necessary for this strategy to provide a satisfying lifestyle in retirement.

Long before thinking about writing this book, I researched many different savings withdrawal systems and created a computerized spreadsheet program to help me plan for my retirement and help me organize my thoughts. I wanted a computer program that allowed me to calculate the effects of a variety of what-if scenarios and help me choose a savings withdrawal system that I would be most comfortable with. I wanted a program that could analyze various spending budgets, determine how much could be safely withdrawn from available savings (without running out of money under various time horizons), and help track progress.

The current version of the spreadsheet program, which was the basis of my previously published workbook, is available for free when you purchase this workbook. It includes the necessary worksheets and automates much of the data input and number crunching, saving you time. It has gone through many revisions and improvements in the years since it was created.

For those of you who are familiar with computer spreadsheets, I urge you to get It before you start using the worksheets in Chapter 11. For those of you not familiar with spreadsheets, I created a computer file containing all the worksheets so you can print them out and use them each year. See the Afterword section at the end of the book on how to get them.

A common issue when using a typical retirement savings withdrawal system is that the suggested withdrawal percentage is usually based on a worst-case scenario. That is, the recommended percentage is one that, in the past, would have allowed you to weather the worst stock market down period in the last 50 to 90 years, if it occurs again during your retirement. While it is considered safe to assume the worst, what often happens during retirement is that the markets perform better than the worst-case scenario. The four withdrawal systems that follow, all assume worst case or near worst case scenarios when testing or back testing the results with historical data.

The 4% Withdrawal System

This system, known as the 4% Rule, is probably the most recognized, and until recent years, was among the most widely recommended savings withdrawal system by most financial planners. It is simple to apply based on how long you would like your savings to last. It is based on a groundbreaking study published in 1994 by Bengen. The original study suggested that 4%

would be a safe withdrawal percent to use at the start of a 30-year retirement based on a worst-case scenario using historical data and having a 95% probability of success.

At the start of your retirement, you decide how long you would like your savings to last and how much of your savings you are willing to spend over the length of your retirement. A look-up table is used to determine the starting withdrawal percentage. At the start of a 38-year retirement, for example, it uses a 3.4% withdrawal rate which when multiplied by the amount of savings you have available at the start of your retirement, arrives at a starting withdrawal amount. This becomes the amount you can withdraw during the first year of retirement. You then increase that amount each year by the previous year inflation rate.

If you started your retirement later in life and wanted your retirement to last 25 years, it uses a 4.7% starting withdrawal rate. The simplicity of this system is that regardless of how your investments perform in subsequent years you just withdraw the previous year's amount and increase it by the previous year inflation rate. It provides a stable annual spending amount that only varies by the inflation rate.

The average annual gain of your investments over the course of your retirement will have a significant affect. Some studies suggest the 4% starting withdrawal rate at the start of a 30 plus year retirement is too high based on the expectation that future investment gains will average less than the historical average. However, those studies were based on worst case scenarios and other studies have shown that most of the time a starting withdrawal rate of 4.0% is very conservative over a 30-year retirement.

Also, the inflation rate has a significant effect on withdrawals over time, and therefore, how long your savings will last. The annual inflation rate has averaged 2.6% over the last 30 years and 3.6% over the last 40 years. If, however the previous year's inflation rate is higher than 3% I suggest you should limit the annual adjustment for inflation to be 3% max and adjust your spending. This should lower your withdrawal amount slightly to prevent the possibility of running out of money later in retirement due to inflation averaging higher than 3%. Appendix III Table 5A lists historical financial data including inflation rates of the last 50 years and how the stock and Bond markets have performed.

Although the 4% system provides short-term spending stability, the major disadvantage of the 4% system, and the reason this system is falling out of favor with many financial planners, is that the long-term effect on your investments is unpredictable. One of the reasons is, it does not allow a reduction in withdrawals if your investments perform poorly over the course of your entire retirement horizon, and thus ***It Does Not Prevent You from Running Out of Money Earlier Than Planned.***

Without adjusting annual withdrawal amounts based on how your investments are performing, your investments could grow slowly over time to a significant amount which would be left unspent during your retirement. If your investments perform poorly over an extended period, it could also be depleted before you had planned on.

Remember that the basis for the 4% system is that the starting withdrawal amount once determined does not change from year to year except for inflation adjustments. It assumes future investment gains and losses over the course of your retirement will perform similar to the worst-case historical performance. The impact that inflation rates and average investment gains have on your retirement can be significant and are discussed in the next chapter.

Even if you decide against using this withdrawal system, it at least provides a conservative rule of thumb in determining how much savings and investments you may need to retire. You estimate your desired annual spending amount to achieve the lifestyle you want, then subtract your estimated after-tax retirement income, and then divide that amount by 4% (or multiply it by 25) to arrive at the amount of savings and investments you may need at the start of your retirement.

The 1/N Withdrawal System

This savings withdrawal system determines the amount you can safely withdraw each year based on the remaining years you have left in retirement. This ensures that your savings will last the length of time you choose.

In the 1/N withdrawal method, the 'N' is equal to the number of years remaining between your current age and the age you have chosen for your savings to be depleted. You determine this number and it is recalculated each year because you have one less year remaining. This results in a higher percentage being withdrawn from your savings each year.

As an example, if you are currently 71 at the beginning of the year and you want your savings to last until age 95 you have 24 years of withdrawals remaining. At the beginning of each year you determine the value of your savings at the end of the previous year. This represents the current value of your savings you are willing to spend over the remaining length of your retirement. You then divide this amount by 24 to determine the amount you can safely withdraw this year. The next year you would have 23 years remaining, so you divide the then available savings value by 23 to determine your withdrawal amount, and so on.

Notice that each year you are dividing your savings by a smaller number which translates to an increasing percentage each year. Normally, withdrawing a higher percentage each year is considered possibly unsafe, as it may result in your savings being eventually depleted. However, using a 1/N withdrawal method typically assumes spending most, if not all the available savings, so large withdrawal percentages near the end of your retirement are not a concern. If you had 2 years to live, then what would a 'safe' withdrawal percentage be? Since you know your savings must only last two years you could safely withdraw 50%.

The advantage of this system is that you cannot outlive your savings unless you live beyond the years you chose for your savings to last. A possible disadvantage of the 1/N strategy is that it suggests a withdrawal amount that is much less in the early years of retirement and much more in the later years. Some studies have shown that you may spend less as you age, especially if you are in reasonably good health or have good medical insurance. You may wish to spend more in the early stages of retirement when you are more active with hobby and travel expenses.

Another possible disadvantage of the 1/N strategy is the amount you withdraw each year will vary with how well your investments did the previous year, so in a significant down year you may have to significantly reduce spending. This will require that you have a flexible spending budget with significant discretionary expenses that can be reduced. As an example, a 20% stock market down year could result in your savings being down 20% or more which could result in you having to reduce spending by 20% or more than the amount you spent in the previous year.

To reduce the possible swings in spending from year to year, some advisers suggest setting limits on how much you need to reduce spending and cap how much more you can spend in good years. See Chapter 10 for details on how this can affect the success of your plan and smooth out year to year withdrawal variability.

The 1/N strategy's annual withdrawal % is not affected by inflation or the average annual investment gain because the withdrawal amount it suggests you take uses the actual value of your available savings at the end of the previous year. This assumes your spending budget for the coming year has been adjusted for expected spending changes, including changes based on increases due to inflation.

The RMD Withdrawal System

This system is based on a table created by the IRS to determine the Required Minimum Distribution from tax advantage accounts like 401K and traditional IRA's. It is based on life expectancy tables. Even if you do not have any tax advantage accounts, the theory behind the table can still apply and some financial planners recommend this system as a conservative withdrawal system for retirees.

The lookup table used in this book was adjusted from a starting age of 70 used by the IRS table, to a starting age of 62 and is based on the same life expectancy tables used by the IRS.

The RMD withdrawal system is easy to apply and allows the withdrawal percentage to increase each year as your remaining life expectancy decreases. You take the value of your available savings at the end of the previous year then divide it by the number that you look up in the RMD withdrawal table based on your age at the beginning of the year.

Like the 1/N withdrawal system a potential disadvantage is the amount you withdraw each year will vary with how well your investments did the previous year. See Chapter 10 for details on how you might be able to smooth out year-to-year withdrawal variability.

Also, like the 1/N strategy the annual withdrawal % is not affected by inflation or the average annual investment gain because the suggested withdrawal amount uses the actual value of available savings at the end of the previous year and assumes your spending budget is adjusted for real inflation each year.

The advantage of this system is that you cannot outlive your savings. However, it is not designed to deplete your savings at the end of the age you choose like the 1/N and VPW withdrawal systems, because even at age 95 at the beginning of the year, it suggests a withdrawal rate of 12.4%. Due to its conservative withdrawals in the later years of retirement it most likely will leave money at the end of your retirement which depending on how well your investment gains did, could be a significant amount that you could have spent during retirement.

The Variable Percentage Withdrawal System:

Known simply as the VPW withdrawal system, this is a withdrawal method that adjusts to retirement length, asset allocation, and investment returns during retirement. It attempts to combine the best ideas of the constant-dollar, constant-percentage, and 1/N systems to allow you to spend your savings using withdrawals that have been adjusted by market returns. By adjusting your withdrawal amounts based on how well your investments did the previous year, it is designed like the 1/N and RMD systems so you cannot outlive your savings unless you live beyond the years you chose for your savings to last.

The VPW withdrawal system is easy to apply and allows the withdrawal percentage to increase each year as your remaining life expectancy decreases. You take the value of your investments at the end of the previous year and then multiply it by the suggested withdrawal percentage that you look up in the VPW withdrawal table based on the years remaining in your plan and the stock to bond percentage reflected in your investments.

Although the VPW withdrawal percentage increase each year as you age, unlike the 1/N based only on years left, or the RMD which uses only life expectancy actuary tables as you age, the VPW system uses historical market performance data and computer simulations to test reliability, similar to the approach used by the 4% system. The big difference is that unlike the 4% system, the VPW system withdrawals adjusts each year based on how your investments performed the previous year thus allowing a higher percentage to be withdrawn each year than the 4% withdrawal system.

The withdrawal percent you use in the look-up table is based on selecting a conservative stock to bond ratio of 20/80, a moderate 40/60, a more aggressive 60/40, or a much more aggressive 80/20. The percent you can withdraw increases as the ratio increases because higher stock ratios should result in improved investment performance over the length of your retirement, but at higher risk, so the withdrawal % it suggests reflects this. See Appendix III Table 5B for the impact that the years remaining and stock to bond ratios have on the VPW withdrawal percentages.

Like the 1/N and RMD withdrawal methods a possible disadvantage of the VPW withdrawal system is your annual withdrawal amounts will always fluctuate with your year-end investment values. Setting limits on how much you can reduce spending and cap how much more you can spend in good years will reduce spending variability. See Chapter 10 for more details on how this can affect the success of your plan and smooth out year-to-year withdrawal variability.

Credit must be given to the group of Bogleheads® that collaboratively developed and improved this savings withdrawal system. I highly recommend going to their website www.bogleheads.org for more information.

Chapter 9

Compare Savings Withdrawal Systems

In this chapter we will compare the effects that the four savings withdrawal systems have on a hypothetical 65-year-old starting retirement with total spendable savings of $500,000 and wanting it to last until age 95, or 30 years of withdrawals. It compares a 3% average annual inflation to a 4% annual inflation rate for the 4% withdrawal system, which is the only withdrawal system impacted by the inflation rate. It compares a 20/80, 40/60, and 60/40 stock to bond investment ratios for the VPW system which is the only withdrawal system that uses different withdrawal rates based on the stock to bond ratio. It will also show the impact that an average annual investment gain of 3.5%, 4.5%, 5.5%, and 6.5% will have over 30 years on all four withdrawal systems.

This comparison is for illustrative purposes only and represents a summary of the results that were generated using a spreadsheet program that was developed several years ago to do What-If comparisons of the four withdrawal systems. It is important to note that the program assumes that the average annual gains studied average that amount every year in retirement, but of course we know this does not happen in real life. The sequence in which the annual gains or losses occur can have a dramatic effect on your retirement plan and the results presented in this chapter.

However, I believe the analysis presented in this chapter is useful in illustrating the differences that the four withdrawal systems have under the same set of assumptions. See Appendix III Table 5B for the annual withdrawal percentages used for each of the withdrawal systems. See the Afterword section at the end of this book if you are interested in obtaining the spreadsheet program to analyze your own retirement plan.

Total withdrawn over 30 years

Table 1A at the end of this chapter shows how much each system would withdraw over the entire 30-year period under differing average annual investment gains. Notice that the 1/N withdrawal system results in the largest total amount withdrawn over 30 years. This is because the 1/N system withdraws a significantly less amount in the early years of retirement, as shown in table 1C, compared to the other systems and thus allows for a larger savings balance to grow over time.

The VPW system is impacted by the stock to bond ratio which affects total average annual investment gains. As the stock to bond ratio increases, the average gains over 30 years should increase as well but of course with more risk. The program automatically adjusts the average gain that is input to reflect the historical differences in various stock to bond ratios. For comparison purposes I show the impact that a 20/80, 40/60, and 60/40 ratio would have on total withdrawals over 30 years. As can be seen, the 40/60 and 60/40 ratios withdraw the second most amount next to the 1/N system.

Notice the RMD withdrawal system withdraws significantly less over the entire retirement withdrawal period compared to the 1/N because its withdrawals are much more conservative in the later years, and it most likely will leave a considerable amount at the end of your retirement as Table 1B shows.

Notice that the 4% Withdrawal system's total withdrawals peak at $970,000 with a 3% annual inflation rate and peaks at $1,144,000 with a 4% annual inflation rate. This is because the amount drawn each year is only adjusted for the inflation rate, so unless it runs out of money early due to poor annual investment gains, it peaks at 30 years, in this example, if the average annual gain is 4.5%. With a 4% annual inflation rate it peaks with a 5.6% or higher average annual gain.

Amount of Savings after 30 years

Table 1B looks at what $500,000 at the start of a 30-year retirement would be at the end of 30 years, for each of the four withdrawal systems, under differing average annual gains. The 4% withdrawal system in table 1B shows that it is significantly impacted by how the investments performs over time and the inflation rate. This could result in either running out of savings earlier than planned or end up with significant savings after 30 years.

As an example, Table 1B shows that if the 4% withdrawal system averages a 3.5% average annual gain over 30 years, which is worst case, and the inflation rate averages 3%, you could run out of money by age 91, or 4 years earlier than planned. If the inflation rate averages 4%, you could run out of money by age 88, or 7 years earlier. If it averages an annual 4.5% gain and the inflation rate is 4%, you could also run out of money by age 91. However, if inflation averages near the historical average and investment gains average a conservative 6.5%, you could end up with $355,000 to $665,000 that you were not able to spend for a more enjoyable retirement!

Notice that the 1/N, RMD, and VPW withdrawal systems, regardless of investment performance, never run out of money over the length of time you chose for your savings to last. However, the suggested annual withdrawal amount is based on the value of your investments at the end of the previous year so depending on how well your investments performed, you may have had to significantly reduce withdrawals and spending during investment down years.

Note that the RMD withdrawal system like the 4% withdrawal system, is not designed to deplete your savings at the end of the age you choose like the 1/N and VPW withdrawal systems. This is because even at age 95 at the beginning of the year, the RMD withdrawal system suggests a withdrawal rate of only 12.4%. Due to its conservative withdrawals in the later years of retirement, most likely it will leave a significant amount that could have been spent during retirement.

Withdrawals in the early years versus later years

Table 1C compares the amount withdrawn during the first 10 years of retirement to the amount withdrawn in the last 10 years of a 30-year retirement, for each of the four withdrawal systems under differing average annual gains. The VPW withdrawal system withdraws the most in the first 10 years of retirement because the withdrawal percentages that it suggests are higher at the start of retirement than the other systems. However, because it withdraws more money early, your savings depletes slightly faster and thus will grow more slowly over time.

The 4% withdrawal system is designed to withdraw the same amount regardless of how much your investments gain, but as you can see, at a low average annual gain of 3.5% it runs out of money before 30 years, which reduces the amount available in the last 10 years of retirement. The 1/N withdrawal system withdraws the least in the first 10 years but by far the most in the last 10 years. As previously mentioned, it has the lowest starting withdrawal percentages and the highest in the later years.

If we look at the amount withdrawn in the first 10 years compared to the last 10 years, as a percent of the total withdrawn over 30 years, and using a 3% inflation rate and 5.5% average annual investment gain, the 4% withdrawal system withdraws 24% of the total in the first 10 years and 44% in the last 10 years, the 1/N system withdraws 18% and 52% respectively, the RMD system withdraws 21% and 45% respectively, and the VPW system withdraws 26% and 41% respectively with a 40/60 stock to bond ratio.

Key Takeaways

From the 4% Withdrawal System:

- Simple to understand and use.

- Steady annual withdrawal amounts make budgeting easier.

- The only withdrawal system presented that does not depend on how well or how poorly your investments perform.

- Does not allow a reduction in withdrawals if your investments perform poorly over the course of your entire retirement horizon.

- Does not prevent you from running out of money earlier than planned.

- Could result in you underspending in retirement if your investments perform better than worst-case historical averages.

From the 1/N Withdrawal System:

- Depending on how well your investments perform the year before, the resulting variable annual withdrawal amounts may make adjusting your spending and budgeting more difficult.

- Depending on how your investments perform over the course of your retirement could result in you having to spend less in the early years of retirement leaving more for the later years.

- Will prevent you from running out of money before you wanted to.

- Results in the largest total amount withdrawn over 30 years. This is because it withdraws significantly less in the early years of retirement compared to the other systems and thus allows for a larger portfolio balance to grow over time.

From the RMD Withdrawal System:

- Depending on how well your investments perform the year before, the resulting variable annual withdrawal amounts may make adjusting your spending and budgeting more difficult.

- Depending on how your investments perform over the course of your entire retirement could result in you having to spend less in the early years of retirement leaving more for the later years.

- Will prevent you from running out of money before you wanted to.

- Is not designed to deplete your savings at the end of the age you choose. This is because even at age 95 at the beginning of the year, the RMD withdrawal system suggests a withdrawal rate of only 12.4%.

- Due to its conservative withdrawal percentages in the later years of retirement, most likely it will leave a significant amount that could have been spent during retirement.

From the VPW Withdrawal System:

- Depending on how well your investments perform the year before, the resulting variable annual withdrawal amounts may make adjusting your spending and budgeting more difficult.

- Will prevent you from running out of money before you wanted to.

- Is designed to deplete your savings at the age you chose.

- Next to the 1/N system the VPW system withdraws the most over 30 years with a stock to bond ratio of 40/60 or higher.

- Withdraws the most in the first 10 years of retirement because the withdrawal percentages that it suggests are higher at the start of retirement than the other systems. However, because it withdraws more money early, the value of your investments is reduced slightly faster and thus will grow more slowly over time. This system may be preferred by those that are more comfortable spending more in the early years and less in the later years.

Table 1A

Avg Annual Gain	Total withdrawn after 30 years starting with $500,000						
	4% System		1/N System	RMD System	VPW System		
	3% Inflation	4% Inflation			20/80	40/60	60/40
3.50%	$787,000	$758,000	**$860,000**	$706,000	$752,000	$796,000	$832,000
4.50%	$970,000	$904,000	**$1,017,000**	$825,000	$853,000	$920,000	$978,000
5.50%	$970,000	$1,139,000	**$1,207,000**	$969,000	$972,000	$1,071,000	$1,157,000
6.50%	$970,000	$1,144,000	**$1,439,000**	$1,143,000	$1,111,000	$1,252,000	$1,379,000

Table 1B

Avg Annual Gain	Amount of Savings after 30 years starting with $500,000						
	4% System		1/N System	RMD System	VPW System		
	3% Inflation	4% Inflation			20/80	40/60	60/40
3.50%	**$0 after 26 yrs.**	**$0 after 23 yrs.**	$0	$200,000	$0	$0	$0
4.50%	**$0 after 30 yrs.**	**$0 after 26 yrs.**	$0	$264,000	$0	$0	$0
5.50%	$276,000	$0	$0	$348,000	$0	$0	$0
6.50%	$665,000	$355,000	$0	$458,000	$0	$0	$0

Table 1C

First 10 years withdrawals compared to last 10 years of a 30 year retirement

Avg. Annual Gain	4% System				1/N System		RMD System	
	3% Annual Inflation		4% Annual Inflation					
	First 10 years	Last 10 years	First 10 years	Last 10 years	First 10 years	Last 10 years	First 10 years	Last 10 years
3.50%	$234,000	$239,000	$245,000	$151,000	$195,000	$389,000	$186,000	$275,000
4.50%	$234,000	$422,000	$245,000	$297,000	$205,000	$494,000	$194,000	$348,000
5.50%	$234,000	$422,000	$245,000	$532,000	$214,000	$626,000	$204,000	$440,000
6.50%	$234,000	$422,000	$245,000	$536,000	$225,000	$792,000	$213,000	$556,000

Avg. Annual Gain	VPW System					
	20/80		40/60		60/40	
	First 10 years	Last 10 years	First 10 years	Last 10 years	First 10 years	Last 10 years
3.50%	$238,000	$263,000	$255,000	$276,000	$275,000	$279,000
4.50%	$247,000	$322,000	$266,000	$349,000	$289,000	$364,000
5.50%	$257,000	$395,000	$278,000	$442,000	$303,000	$474,000
6.50%	$267,000	$484,000	$291,000	$558,000	$319,000	$616,000

Chapter 10

Set Spending Limits

If you chose to use the 4% withdrawal system as your withdrawal method you can skip this chapter and go to Chapter 11, since this approach does not allow your withdrawal amounts to vary each year except to accommodate for inflation, and therefore is not based on how your investments are performing year to year.

With the other withdrawal systems, the amount you can withdraw each year will depend on the value of your investments at the end of the previous year. To reduce the potential for significant changes in spending from year to year, this chapter explains the benefits of using one of three spending limit systems.

The best system to use is to not set any limits and just adjust your spending up or down depending on the performance of your investments the previous year. This provides the greatest chance that you will not have to make significant cuts to your spending in the later years of your retirement even if a series of poor performing investment years occur over an extended period. This approach requires a lot of discretionary spending flexibility and the ability to reduce spending significantly in poor performing years. Many of us do not have this amount of spending flexibility, especially if we experience several years in a row of poor performing investments.

As previously stated, a 20% drop in your savings could result in a 20% or more drop in the suggested withdrawal amount from the previous year. Since 1970 the S&P 500 index of stocks has fallen 20% or more only 3 times with the worst years having dropped 38.5% in 2008, 29.7% in 1974, 23.4% in 2002, 17.4% in 1973, and 13.0% in 2001. Remember that future market performance may be better or worse than historical performances. (See Appendix III Table 5A for historical financial performance data).

Setting Lower & Upper Spending Limits

If like many people your discretionary spending is limited, then setting a lower spending limit percent based on the amount you can afford to reduce spending will help reduce the impact of down years. Keep in mind that the lower the lower limit percent amount is that you set, you must also lower the upper limit percent so that in up years you do not spend all the extra that may be available, leaving some of it to help offset the down years.

This spending limit approach was based on a study by Vanguard describing the benefits of setting a ceiling and floor amount to spending. I changed the definition of ceiling to setting a **Lower Limit,** that suggests spending will not drop below this limit, and changed the definition of floor to setting an **Upper Limit**, that suggests spending will not go above this limit.

Worksheets 5, 6, or 7 at the end of the next chapter are where you can set the Upper & Lower limit percentages. If your spending is flexible enough, I suggest setting the lower limit to as high as 15% to ensure greater success if it becomes necessary to reduce spending. If you used Worksheet 1 to establish your spending budget and you calculated the Budget Flexibility % at the bottom of the Worksheet, I would suggest using a similar percentage for the lower limit or a percentage reduction you are comfortable with.

It is important to set the upper limit percentage amount to be equal to or lower than the lower limit so that in a good year you limit how much extra you can spend to help balance the up years with the down years. Keep in mind that setting lower and upper spending limits does not prevent having to reduce spending more than the lower limit suggests if a substantial decline in your savings occurs over several periods during retirement.

Creating a separate reserve fund

Although this is the system I use, I do not recommend this method unless you are comfortable with how it works, are willing to keep a record of the balance amount and have some spending flexibility. The reason I created it, and began using it in 2014, was to provide more control and flexibility over how you spend your money from one year to the next compared to the fixed spending limits. If the reserve fund is positive and you want to spend more that year than the withdrawal system determines, you can use it to pay for a special or unplanned expense.

The *reserve fund* is separate from your *emergency fund* and both should not be considered as part of your savings that is used to calculate the suggested withdrawal amount. The reserve fund amount will reduce your withdrawal amount slightly by the percentage of the reserve fund amount divided by the total available savings amount. You decide on the reserve fund starting amount. I would suggest starting the reserve fund with an amount equal to 25% of the previous year's spending amount.

Using the example of a 65-year-old retiree with $500,000 in available savings, a 5% withdrawal rate, and having spent $55,000 the previous year, he would start the reserve fund at $13,750 (25% x $55,000). He would then subtract the reserve fund amount from the previous year-ending available savings amount prior to calculating the current year withdrawal amount. In this example, the withdrawal amount only drops $687 from $25,000 to $24,313 or 2.8%.

This reserve fund can be an actual separate account with actual money in it, or it can be a hypothetical reserve fund. Mine is hypothetical which required setting up a record keeping system to track the amount each year. In either case, you would add to or reduce the fund depending on the difference between the *desired* spending amount and the calculated *suggested* amount based on the withdrawal system you selected.

If the previous year investment performance was poor, and the suggested withdrawal amount is less than your desired amount, you must decide how much to reduce the reserve fund and use it to make up for some of the spending shortfall and how much to reduce spending.

If the suggested withdrawal amount is greater than your desired amount, decide how much of the difference you want to add to spending and how much to save and put into the reserve fund to save for future down years. Worksheet 3 "Total Spendable Value of Your Portfolio" includes an entry for this optional reserve fund.

Keep in mind that if the reserve fund gets depleted due to several poor performing years you will have to decide to either re-fund it, reduce spending further, or switch to using upper and lower spending limits.

This chapter may seem confusing or appear difficult to understand or implement but I believe it will make more sense and be easier to apply after reading the next chapter.

Chapter 11

Calculate Your Safe Withdrawal Amount

This chapter will answer the two questions raised at the beginning; *How much can I safely spend in retirement each year* and *If I need or want to spend more than my expected income, how much of my savings can I safely withdraw each year so that I do not outlive my savings.*

If you have not requested and received the companion computerized spreadsheet program, now would be a good time to do so. With the program you can fill out the worksheets faster and/or do What-If analysis and comparisons easily.

Worksheets 1, 2, and 3 will be used along with one of the worksheets you decide to use at the end of this chapter to calculate your safe spending and savings withdrawal amounts. It is important that they are as accurate as possible and reflect your current thinking regarding your retirement spending budget, your retirement after-tax income, and available savings. You should review them carefully and revise them accordingly before proceeding to the next step.

How long do you want your plan to last?

More specifically, how long do you want your savings to last to support your retirement plan. If you and/or your partner are reasonably healthy, a safe age to use is 95, with 100 not unreasonable with the advances being made in medicine Today. Depending on what life expectancy table or study you use, a reasonably healthy 65-year-old male on average will live to age 88 and has a 10 to 20% chance of making it to age 95. A reasonably healthy female can expect to live about 2.5 years longer.

The longevity of an opposite sex couple in reasonably good health, increases the chances of one of you making it to age 95 to 20 to 40%. Since there is better than a 10% chance of living to 95, it is a reasonable, conservative, and less risky age to use.

But those are just averages. "About one out of every three 65-year-olds today will live past age 90, and about one out of seven will live past age 95," according to the Social Security Administration.

Worksheets 4, 5, 6, or 7

After selecting the retirement withdrawal system that you are most comfortable, you will need to complete the appropriate Worksheet, either 4, 5, 6 or 7 at the end of this chapter. This is probably the hardest and most important decision you will need to make to create a successful retirement spending and withdrawal plan.

You may want to reread chapters 8 & 9 or seek additional professional help so that you are comfortable with the system you or your advisor choose.

You may want to compare withdrawal systems by filling out more than one worksheet to see how they compare. If you have not requested and received the free companion computerized spreadsheet program, now would be a good time to do so. With the program you can fill out the worksheets faster and/or do What-If analysis and comparisons easily.

The calculations are limited to a maximum of 38 years of withdrawals so depending on the age you enter for the first year in retirement you could enter an ending age up to 38 years from then. As an example, if you start your retirement at age 60 you could enter a plan ending age of 98, if you want your savings to last that long. Obviously the longer you want your savings to last the less you can withdraw each year. Conversely, the risk of outliving your savings goes up as you shorten the length.

You begin by entering the age you want to begin withdrawing retirement savings, the age you want your savings to last to, your desired annual spending amount, your annual after-tax income, and the total investment amounts that were all determined in Worksheets 1,2 and 3. The selected worksheet, either 4, 5, 6, or 7 will then determine how much if any shortfall there is that needs to be withdrawn from your savings. It will then determine if your desired spending plan is achievable compared to what the worksheet suggests you can spend.

If the shortfall is less than the suggested withdrawal amount based on the withdrawal system you choose, your plan is good and may even allow you to increase your spending. Conversely, if the shortfall is greater than the suggested withdrawal amount, you may have to reduce your spending plan, reduce the length of time you want your savings to last, or increase your savings by possibly working longer.

The next chapter will explore opportunities to reduce spending. Even if your suggested safe spending amount is enough to meet your needs, you may want to reduce your fixed costs to have more spending flexibility. This may also allow you to spend in ways that improve your happiness in retirement such as more travel or leisure activities.

Note if you choose the 4% Withdrawal System you only need to fill out worksheets 1, 2, and 3 at the beginning of your retirement and not annually, but I recommend doing it at the beginning of every year so you can track how your plan is doing over time. The other three withdrawal systems require recalculating your withdrawal amount at the beginning of each year based on the value of your available savings ending the previous December 31st.

If you choose the RMD withdrawal system, it will most likely leave money at the end of your plan, due to its conservative nature as explained in Chapters 8 and 9. If you allocated money to be used as a cushion or hedge that you live longer than planned in worksheet 3, you might consider reducing or eliminating the amount, because this amount is subtracted each year from your available savings amount before the withdrawal amount is calculated. This reduces your annual withdrawal amount that you could have spent.

It is very important that you do not attempt to change withdrawal systems or change expected investment gains or other variables used from one year to the next without a thorough understanding of the implications those changes may have on the success of your retirement.

CAUTION: As stated previously, the future may contain scenarios that are better or worse than anything considered by this book. It is also important to remember that, despite the sophistication of the methods used, this book makes several simplifying assumptions. Note that the Suggested Withdrawal amounts are just that, Suggestions, and are designed to prevent you from significantly over or under spending your savings. It is highly recommended that you seek additional guidance in developing a retirement plan with which you will be most comfortable.

Worksheet 4: Instructions for Using the 4% Withdrawal System

Line No. 1: Enter Current Year.

Line No. 2: Enter Current Age at start of current year.

Line No. 3: Enter Age at which your savings should be depleted.

Line No. 4: Subtract Line 2 from Line 3 to get years remaining for your savings to last.

Line No. 5: Enter "Total All Expenses" from Worksheet 1.

Line No. 6: Enter "Total Annual After-Tax Income" from Worksheet 2.

Line No. 7: Enter "Total Portfolio amount available to spend in retirement" from Worksheet 3.

Line No. 8: Subtract Line 6 from Line 5 to get Desired Withdrawal Amount.

Line No. 9: Enter the number found in the "Divisor" column Table 2 based on years left, as indicated in line 4.

Line No. 10: Divide Line 7 by Line 9 to get Suggested First Year Withdrawals.

Line No. 11: Subtract Line 8 from Line 10. This will be the amount that can be added to your desired spending budget if it is a positive number or subtracted from your desired spending budget if it is a negative number.

Line No. 12: Add Lines 6, 8, & 11 to arrive at the amount you can safely spend in the first year of your retirement.

Remember this Worksheet is only used once at the start of your retirement. The amount on line 10 which is the Suggested first year withdrawal amount will then be increased for inflation each year thereafter.

Worksheet 4: Using the 4% Withdrawal System

Use this Worksheet only At The Beginning of your first year of retirement
See Note at bottom of this Worksheet

Line No.		
1		Current Year
2		Current Age at Start of the year
3		Age Savings should End or be depleted
4		Years you want your Savings to last
5		Desired Total Spending for Year
6		Estimated Total Annual After Tax Income
7		Total Spendable Value of your Portfolio at start of retirement
8		Desired Withdrawal Amount
9		Suggested "Divisor" number from Table 2
10		Suggested First Year Withdrawal
11		Amount above or below the Desired Withdrawal amount
12		Suggested Amount You Could Safely Spend in The First Year Of Your Retirement

Note: In subsequent years increase Line 10 amount by the previous year's inflation rate and add it to your expected income for the year to arrive at the new safe spending amount.

Table 2: 4% Withdrawal System

Years Left	Divisor	Equivalent %	Years Left	Divisor	Equivalent %
38	29.4	3.4%	19	16.7	6.0%
37	28.9	3.5%	18	16.0	6.3%
36	28.3	3.5%	17	15.2	6.6%
35	27.7	3.6%	16	14.4	7.0%
34	27.1	3.7%	15	13.6	7.4%
33	26.4	3.8%	14	12.8	7.8%
32	25.8	3.9%	13	11.9	8.4%
31	25.2	4.0%	12	11.1	9.0%
30	24.5	4.1%	11	10.2	9.8%
29	23.9	4.2%	10	9.4	10.7%
28	23.2	4.3%	9	8.5	11.8%
27	22.5	4.4%	8	7.6	13.1%
26	21.8	4.6%	7	6.7	14.9%
25	21.1	4.7%	6	5.8	17.3%
24	20.4	4.9%	5	4.9	20.6%
23	19.7	5.1%	4	3.9	25.6%
22	19.0	5.3%	3	3.0	33.9%
21	18.2	5.5%	2	2.0	50.5%
20	17.5	5.7%	1	1.0	100.0%

Worksheet 5: Instructions for using the 1/N Withdrawal System

Line No. 1: Enter Current Year.

Line No. 2: Enter Current Age at start of current year.

Line No. 3: Enter Age at which your savings should be depleted.

Line No. 4: Subtract Line 2 from Line 3 to get years remaining for your savings to last.

Line No. 5: Enter "Total All Expenses" from Worksheet 1.

Line No. 6: Enter "Total Annual After-Tax Income" from Worksheet 2.

Line No. 7: Enter "Total Portfolio amount available to spend in retirement" from Worksheet 3.

Line No. 8: Subtract Line 6 from Line 5 to get Desired Withdrawal Amount.

Line No. 9: Divide Line 7 by Line 4 to get the Suggested Annual Withdrawal.

Line No. 10: Subtract Line 8 from Line 9. This will be the amount that can be added to your desired spending budget if it is a positive number or subtracted from your desired spending budget if it is a negative number.

Line No. 11: Skip if no spending limits are needed or a reserve fund is used, otherwise set the spending limit to a percentage that you are comfortable with. The higher the better. If you are comfortable using the Budget Flexibility % calculated at the bottom of worksheet 1 use this percentage. **Enter the percentage as a negative number.** See Chapter 10 on setting limits if needed.

Line No. 12: If a percentage is entered on line 11 multiply it by line 5. Should be a negative number.

Line No. 13: Skip if no spending limits are needed or a reserve fund is used, otherwise set it to a percentage equal to that on line 11 but no more than 15%. **Enter the percentage as a positive number**. See Chapter 10 on setting limits if needed.

Line No. 14: If a percentage is entered on line 13 multiply it by line 5. Should be a positive number.

Line No. 15: If you set Lower and Upper Spending limits and line 10 is negative, then enter the lessor amount between line 10 and line 12. Conversely if line 10 is a positive number, enter the lessor amount between line 10 and line 14.

If no spending limit is needed, then enter the amount from line 10. If line 10 is negative enter the amount as a negative number.

If a reserve fund is used, then decide how much of line 10 will be entered as an adjustment to spending. If line 10 is negative decide how much of this amount you want to reduce by using some of your reserve fund if any and enter the reduced amount as a negative amount on line 15. You will then need to reduce your reserve account by the amount you reduced line 10.

Conversely if the amount on line 10 is positive again decide how much if any of this amount you want to use to increase spending and enter this amount as a positive number on line 15. You will then need to add the amount you elected not to spend of line 10, to your reserve account.

Line No. 16: Add Line 5 and line 15 to arrive at the suggested amount you can Safely spend for the year.

Worksheet 5: Using the 1/N Withdrawal System

Line No.		Create at the beginning of each Year
1		Current Year
2		Current Age at Start of the year
3		Age Savings should End or be depleted
4		Years remaining for your Savings to last
5		Desired Total Spending for Year
6		Estimated Total Annual After Tax Income
7		Total Spendable Value of your Portfolio at the beginning of the year
8		Desired Withdrawal Amount
9		Suggested Annual Withdrawal
10		Amount above or below the Desired Withdrawal amount
11		Lower Spending Limit % (See Note below)
12		
13		Upper Spending Limit % (See Note below)
14		
15		Spending Limit Adjustment
16		Suggested Amount You Could Safely Spend for the year

NOTE: If no limits are needed or a reserve fund is used skip lines 11 thru 14
If Lower & Upper spending limit % is used choose these limits
carefully. See Chapter "Set Spending Limits" for more details.

Worksheet 6: Instructions for using the RMD Withdrawal System

Line No. 1: Enter Current Year.

Line No. 2: Enter Current Age at start of current year. Must be 62 or higher.

Line No. 3: Enter "Total All Expenses" from Worksheet 1.

Line No. 4: Enter "Total Annual After-Tax Income" from Worksheet 2.

Line No. 5: Enter "Total Portfolio amount available to spend in retirement" from Worksheet 3.

Line No. 6: Subtract Line 4 from Line 3 to get Desired Withdrawal Amount.

Line No. 7: Enter the "Divisor" number found in Table 3 based on your current age as shown in line 2.

Line No. 8: Divide Line 5 by Line 7 to get the Suggested Annual Withdrawal amount.

Line No. 9: Subtract Line 6 from Line 8. This will be the amount that can be added to your desired spending budget if it is a positive number or subtracted from your desired spending budget if it is a negative number.

Line No. 10: Skip if no spending limits are needed or a reserve fund is used, otherwise set the spending limit to a percentage that you are comfortable with. The higher the better. If you are comfortable using the Budget Flexibility % calculated at the bottom of worksheet 1 use this percentage. **Enter the percentage as a negative number.** See Chapter 10 on setting limits if needed.

Line No. 11: If a percentage is entered on line 10 multiply it by line 3. Should be a negative number.

Line No. 12: Skip if no spending limits are needed or a reserve fund is used, otherwise set it to a percentage equal to that on line 10 but no more than 15%. **Enter the percentage as a positive number**. See Chapter 10 on setting limits if needed.

Line No. 13: If a percentage is entered on line 12 multiply it by line 3. Should be a positive number.

Line No. 14: If you set Lower and Upper Spending limits and line 9 is negative, then enter the lessor amount between line 9 and line 11. Conversely if line 9 is a positive number, enter the lessor amount between line 9 and line 13.

If no spending limit is needed, then enter the amount from line 9. If line 9 is negative enter the amount as a negative number.

If a reserve fund is used, then decide how much of line 9 will be entered as an adjustment to spending. If line 9 is negative decide how much of this amount you want to reduce by using some of your reserve fund if any and enter the reduced amount as a negative amount on line 14. You will then need to reduce your reserve account by the amount you reduced line 9.

Conversely if the amount on line 9 is positive again decide how much if any of this amount you want to use to increase spending and enter this amount as a positive number on line 14. You will then need to add the amount you elected not to spend of line 9, to your reserve account.

Line No. 15: Add Lines 3 and line 14 to arrive at the suggested amount you can Safely spend for the year.

Worksheet 6: Using the RMD Withdrawal System

Create at the beginning of each Year

Line No.		
1		Current Year
2		Current Age. Must be 62 or higher
3		Desired Total Spending for Year
4		Estimated Total Annual After Tax Income
5		Total Spendable Value of your Portfolio at the beginning of the year
6		Desired Withdrawal Amount
7		Suggested Withdrawal Divisor Table 3
8		Suggested Annual Withdrawal
9		Amount above or below the Desired Withdrawal amount
10		Lower Spending Limit % (See Note below)
11		
12		Upper Spending Limit % (See Note below)
13		
14		Spending Limit Adjustment
15		Suggested Amount You Could Safely Spend for the year

NOTE: If no limits are needed or a reserve fund is used skip lines 11 thru 14
If Lower & Upper spending limit % is used choose these limits carefully. See Chapter "Set Spending Limits" for more details.

Table 3: RMD Withdrawal System

Your Age at the beginning of the current year	Withdrawal Divisor	Your Age at the beginning of the current year	Withdrawal Divisor
62	33.8	82	16.3
63	32.9	83	15.5
64	32.0	84	14.8
65	31.1	85	14.1
66	30.2	86	13.4
67	29.2	87	12.7
68	28.3	88	12.0
69	27.4	89	11.4
70	26.5	90	10.8
71	25.6	91	10.2
72	24.7	92	9.6
73	23.8	93	9.1
74	22.9	94	8.6
75	22.0	95	8.1
76	21.2	96	7.6
77	20.3	97	7.1
78	19.5	98	6.7
79	18.7	99	6.3
80	17.9	100	5.9
81	17.1		

Worksheet 7: Instructions for using the VPW Withdrawal System

Line No. 1: Enter Current Year.

Line No. 2: Enter Current Age at start of current year.

Line No. 3: Enter Age at which your savings should be depleted.

Line No. 4: Subtract Line 2 from Line 3 to get years remaining for your savings to last.

Line No. 5: Enter "Total All Expenses" from Worksheet 1.

Line No. 6: Enter "Total Annual After-Tax Income" from Worksheet 2.

Line No. 7: Enter "Total Portfolio amount available to spend in retirement" from Worksheet 3.

Line No. 8: Subtract Line 6 from Line 5 to get Desired Withdrawal Amount.

Line No. 9: Enter the "Divisor" number found in Table 4 based on years left as shown in line 4 and your closest stock to bond ratio at the beginning of the year.

Line No. 10: Divide Line 7 by Line 9 to get the Suggested Annual Withdrawal amount.

Line No. 11: Subtract Line 8 from Line 10. This is the amount above (positive number) or below (negative number) the desired withdrawal amount.

Line No. 12: Skip if no spending limits are needed or a reserve fund is used otherwise, set the spending limit to a percentage that you are comfortable with. The higher the better. If you are comfortable using the Budget Flexibility % calculated at the bottom of worksheet 1 use this percentage. **Enter the percentage as a negative number.** See Chapter 10 on setting limits if needed.

Line No. 13: If a percentage is entered on line 12 multiply it by line 5. Should be a negative number.

Line No. 14: Skip if no spending limits are needed or a reserve fund is used, otherwise set it to a percentage equal to that on line 12 but no more than 15%. **Enter the percentage as a positive number**. See Chapter 10 on setting limits if needed.

Line No. 15: If a percentage is entered on line 14 multiply it by line 5. Should be a positive number.

Line No. 16: If you set Lower and Upper Spending limits and line 11 is negative then enter the lessor amount between line 11 and line 13. Conversely if line 11 is a positive number enter the lessor amount between line 11 and line 15.

If no spending limit is needed, then enter the amount on line 11. If line 11 is negative enter the amount as a negative number.

If a reserve fund is used, then decide how much of line 11 will be entered as an adjustment to spending. If line 11 is negative decide how much of this amount you want to reduce by using some of your reserve fund if any and enter the reduced amount as a negative amount on line 16. You will then need to reduce your reserve account by the amount you reduced line 11.

Conversely if the amount on line 11 is positive again decide how much if any of this amount you want to use to increase spending and enter this amount as a positive number on line 16. You will then need to add the amount you elected not to spend of line 11, to your reserve account.

Line No. 17: Add Line 5 and line 16 to arrive at the suggested amount you can Safely spend for the year.

Worksheet 7: Using the VPW Withdrawal System

	Create at the beginning of each Year	
Line No.		
1		Current Year
2		Current Age at Start of the year
3		Age Savings should End or be depleted
4		Years remaining for your Savings to last
5		Desired Total Spending for Year
6		Estimated Total Annual After Tax Income
7		Total Spendable Value of your Portfolio at the beginning of the year
8		Desired Withdrawal Amount
9		Suggested Withdrawal Divisor Table 4
10		Suggested Annual Withdrawal
11		Amount above or below the Desired Withdrawal amount
12		Lower Spending Limit % (See Note below)
13		
14		Upper Spending Limit % (See Note below)
15		
16		Spending Limit Adjustment
17		Suggested Amount You Could Safely Spend for the year

NOTE: If no limits are needed or a reserve fund is used skip lines 12 thru 15
If Lower & Upper spending limit % is used choose these limits carefully. See Chapter "Set Spending Limits" for more details.

Table 4: VPW Withdrawal System Divisors

Years Left	VPW Stock to Bond ratio			
	20/80	40/60	60/40	80/20
38	25.0	22.7	20.8	19.2
37	25.0	22.7	20.4	18.9
36	24.4	22.2	20.4	18.9
35	23.8	21.7	20.0	18.5
34	23.3	21.3	19.6	18.2
33	22.7	21.3	19.2	17.9
32	22.2	20.8	18.9	17.9
31	21.7	20.4	18.5	17.5
30	21.3	20.0	18.2	17.2
29	20.8	19.6	17.9	16.9
28	20.4	19.2	17.5	16.7
27	20.0	18.5	17.2	16.4
26	19.6	18.2	16.9	15.9
25	18.9	17.9	16.4	15.6
24	18.2	17.2	16.1	15.4
23	17.9	16.7	15.6	14.9
22	17.2	16.4	15.2	14.5
21	16.7	15.6	14.7	14.1
20	15.9	15.2	14.3	13.7
19	15.4	14.7	13.9	13.3
18	14.7	14.1	13.3	12.8
17	14.1	13.5	12.8	12.3
16	13.3	12.8	12.2	11.8
15	12.7	12.2	11.6	11.2
14	12.0	11.6	11.1	10.8
13	11.2	10.9	10.4	10.2
12	10.5	10.2	9.8	9.6
11	9.7	9.5	9.2	8.9
10	9.0	8.8	8.5	8.3
9	8.2	8.0	7.8	7.6
8	7.4	7.2	7.0	6.9
7	6.5	6.4	6.3	6.2
6	5.6	5.6	5.5	5.4
5	4.8	4.7	4.7	4.6
4	3.9	3.8	3.8	3.8
3	2.9	2.9	2.9	2.9
2	2.0	2.0	2.0	2.0
1	1.0	1.0	1.0	1.0

The above table is based on a table Collaboratively developed by a group of Bogleheads®. www.bogleheads.org

Chapter 12

Opportunities to Reduce Spending

If your savings withdrawal system indicates that you will need to reduce spending or you want to shift spending from essential expenses to discretionary spending to do more of what makes you happy, the following may help.

Should You Downsize?

Downsizing your home and moving into a smaller and less expensive property, has many advantages. The most obvious benefit is a financial one. It is one of the biggest and fastest ways to cut your expenses but that is not the only benefit. Here are some compelling reasons to move to a smaller place:

- Selling your home may improve your quality of life and give you more time to pursue hobbies and other interests. You may have needed that large home when you were raising your children, but now that the kids are grown and out on their own, all that space just mean more cleaning and upkeep.

- If your home is worth a lot of money, selling it could free up a lot of cash. Even if you choose to buy a new property, chances are it will be less expensive than the one you previously owned. It costs money to move and get your home ready for sale, but you should end up with more money in the bank.

- If you have a mortgage, your monthly payments are suddenly going to get much smaller. And if you own your home or have built up a substantial amount of equity, you may be able to buy your new home outright. You could then be eligible for a reverse mortgage if you should need the money later in retirement.

- A smaller home will cost less to maintain and insure. Your tax bill is likely to be less as well. Your utility bills will be lower since you would no longer be paying to heat and cool those extra rooms and floors.

- You would also be able to sell your excess stuff and buy less stuff, since you have less room to put it in.

There are also some potential downsides to selling your home in retirement. If you retire during a down housing market, you may not get as much for your home as you had hoped. That could limit the options you have going forward, either forcing you into a smaller home than you need or reducing the amount of money you may have to pursue other interests.

Retirement is a major change in terms of finances, but the change in lifestyle is just as significant. If selling your home and downsizing in retirement is something you are willing to consider, testing it out by renting for a few months may make a lot of sense.

Should you Rent instead of own? Whether to rent or own in retirement is a major decision that should not be taken lightly. Either option could hurt or help your financial security depending on where you live and what your specific needs are.

Owning offers stability, equity and possibly tax benefits, while renting provides more flexibility and liquidity, and you will not have to spend money and time on maintenance like lawn care and snow removal. You will also have predictable housing costs, and not be responsible for most repairs. However, renting in a popular urban area with a rising cost of living could bring increasingly higher rent that could eventually reach an amount you can no longer afford.

Selling your house may free up money that you can invest and can increase your overall income during your retirement years. Investments often grow at a faster rate than real estate appreciates, making it a better use of your money. Also, home ownership puts you at risk of a large unexpected maintenance cost that renting does not do.

Become a one-car household: According to AAA, the average cost of vehicle ownership in 2018 is $9,282 annually. That is a lot of money to spend for transportation. But it can also represent a lot of money saved if you are one-half of a retired couple who downsize from two cars to one. After all, how often do you and your partner use a car at the same time for different errands? You will also gain room in your garage!

Selling a Second Home: If you have a second home, consider selling it before retiring and eliminate a potential drain on your savings. The maintenance and real estate taxes can become too much to maintain. Also, real estate tax laws have been less favorable for second homes. Selling the second home will allow you to use the proceeds to pursue travel and add to your bucket list.

Pay off the mortgage: Many financial planners recommend their clients pay down mortgages while still working so that they are as debt-free as they can be when they retire. It may make sense to pay off your mortgage especially if your investments have become more conservative as you age and are not expected to return much more than the interest you are paying on the mortgage. Paying off the mortgage will also reduce your fixed expenses and give you more spending flexibility when you may need it most.

To cover mortgage payments, retirees frequently withdraw more from their retirement accounts like IRA or 401K, than they would if the mortgage were paid off. Those withdrawals typically trigger more taxes including higher taxes on your social security income, while reducing the amount of money that retirees will have to live on.

Conversely, you may not have the option to pay-off your mortgage without withdrawing a sizeable amount from your IRA or 401K. This could trigger an increase in income taxes including additional tax on your Social Security. As an example, if you withdraw $60,000 from your IRA to pay off your mortgage, you might end up with less than $50,000 after taxes and leave you short of cash for emergencies or future living expenses.

Limit Your Insurance Costs: Many retirees carry unnecessary insurance products that they continue paying for but do not get any value from. Look at raising insurance deductibles on your home and collision on your cars. Consider dropping collision coverage completely on any car whose value is under $5,000. Drop life insurance products and disability insurance when you are no longer working or need to provide for others after you are gone.

You should never feel obligated to buy a warranty for every device and appliance you own. Retirees are often victims of warranty 'scams' for things like TVs and other household goods that lead to unnecessary spending. Salespeople have historically pushed warranties when you purchase an item because they are very profitable to the store.

According to Consumer Reports, extended warranties are almost never worth the money, except possibly a warranty for your smartphone if you are prone to dropping or losing it!

I am a strong believer in self-insuring for those costs that you know the amount you would have to cover and that would not be catastrophic to your retirement. The money you save in not buying insurance coverage over a long period of time will most likely be much more than the occasional loss you had to cover and pay for. Again, these types of policies are huge profit makers for those that offer them.

Some more examples of lucrative policies to avoid are pre-paying for funeral expenses or buying Trip Cancellation insurance when you go on vacation. Cruise lines are notorious for selling expensive trip cancellation policies with low medical coverage and requiring you to pay for the cruise far in advance of disembarking. The way I look at it, if I had to cancel at the last minute, I really did not lose the money I prepaid since it was already spent, I only lost the experience of not taking the cruise and what most likely would have been an enjoyable trip.

However, for costs that could be huge, unknown and could be catastrophic to your retirement finances, it would be wise to buy good quality insurance coverage. Having good health insurance coverage is extremely important, but be careful, especially if you or your spouse are in reasonably good health. Paying extra for low annual out-of-pocket maximums, having low copays or low prescription deductibles, whose costs are predictable or known, may not be worth the increased monthly premium costs in the long run.

Other examples of insurance to consider buying are special policies that cover medical emergencies and emergency transportation or repatriation costs when travelling outside of your medical insurance coverage area, and especially when traveling out of the country. Very reasonable trip medical insurance plans can be purchased that have typical coverages of $50,000 emergency medical and $250,000 to cover emergency transportation or repatriation costs.

Chapter 13

Minimizing Taxes and Maximizing Investment Returns

After you determine how much to withdraw from your investments to support your retirement lifestyle in the new year, you will need to determine which accounts you should withdraw from and in what order. *When* you withdraw money from your investments is not nearly as important as deciding *What investments* need to be sold and in *What Order* to fund your retirement. Withdrawing closer to when you need to spend it may allow your investment to grow longer.

Studies have shown that what types of assets such as cash, stocks, and bonds you withdraw from can have a big impact on how well your investments grow long term. They have also shown that the order in which you withdraw them can have a significant impact on taxes.

What type of assets to Sell?

Historical data suggests that your portfolio value can vary significantly even with the same investments and the same withdrawal rate. It depends on *what* asset classes such as cash, stocks, and bonds you choose to sell. As Warren Buffet once said, "Be Fearful When

Others Are Greedy and Greedy When Others Are Fearful." Buying assets when they are out of favor and selling them when they are in favor seems to make good sense.

As an example, when you need to withdraw money from your investments, sell some of your most appreciated assets. So, in a Bear Market you would cash in your money market and short-term bonds and hold longer term bonds and stocks until a Bull Market returns and then sell longer term bonds and stocks when needed.

Conversely, it does not seem to make sense to live off your conservative cash and bond assets when stock markets are up. Yes, stocks could continue to go up, but they could easily go down since you cannot predict when the bull market ends or retracts. The challenge with this method is finding a reliable indicator, so you do not sell too early or too late in the market cycle. For more information regarding this and other interesting methods of maximizing your returns, See Appendix IV References & Resources Chapter 13.

Using this method also acts as a self-rebalancing mechanism, helping to keep your investments properly diversified. The reason is that as stocks rise in a bull market, your stock ratio increases above your target ratio so when it is time to rebalance you would need to reduce your stock holdings forcing you to sell high. Conversely, as stocks fall in a bear market the ratio falls below your target forcing you to buy stocks at depressed values. This is also true with bonds. The next chapter will explain the importance of rebalancing your investment mix.

In what order should you withdraw?

The order in which you withdraw funds can have a significant effect on income taxes, so the goal should be to try and minimize the impact of taxes while maximizing investment returns.

If you or your spouse have tax differed accounts like IRA's and 401K's (Not Roth IRA's) you may be required by the IRS to withdraw a minimum amount based on your age to avoid a 50% penalty being assessed by the IRS for not withdrawing enough. This is known as the RMD amount or **R**equired **M**inimum **D**istribution amount.

The IRS allowed you to put the money into the tax differed account tax-free but once you reach a certain age, they want those tax dollars back! Always withdraw this amount first to determine if you need to withdraw more from your savings to meet your spending needs.

The rules regarding the age you must start taking the RMD changed with the passing of the SECURE Act which became law on December 20, 2019. You should consult IRS publication 590-B Distributions from

IRA's and a tax specialist if uncomfortable with this topic.

You do not have to spend the RMD amount so long as you pay the income tax due. If it is more than you need, you can invest it in a taxable account. It is important to note that if you only withdraw the minimum RMD required in the early years of retirement, it may push you into a higher income tax bracket in your later years.

Withdrawing more money from accounts subject to RMDs before you must withdraw the RMD during the early years of your retirement helps reduce the amount of your RMDs when you reach the required age to take the RMD. This will lower the tax in your later years but possibly raise the amount of taxes you will pay early in retirement. This may or may not be advantageous, depending on the tax bracket you are currently in versus what bracket you may be in later in retirement.

If additional withdrawals beyond the RMD amount are necessary to meet your spending needs, there are several methods you can use, but each have varying tax consequences. One method to minimize taxes is to first withdraw from your taxable accounts until almost depleted, then from your tax deferred IRA and 401K accounts, and lastly from Roth IRA's. This method works well if you will be in a higher tax bracket in your early years of retirement rather than in your later years.

Conversely, if you think you will be in a higher tax bracket later in your retirement, then withdrawing first from your IRA's or 401K's, then your taxable accounts will make more sense.

Another method is to withdraw a proportional amount between your taxable and tax deferred accounts. A proportional amount is withdrawn from each of your accounts based on the proportion of your retirement savings in each account type. This helps stretch your savings by spreading out the tax advantages that your retirement accounts offer, reducing significant swings in the amount of taxes you pay each year. Using this method should allow you to pay a similar amount in taxes each year. This also makes budgeting for taxes easier. This method works well if you do not think your tax bracket will vary much in retirement.

As an example, suppose you have $500,000 in total investments to draw from of which $100,000 is in taxable savings and brokerage accounts, $325,000 in a 401K and IRA and $75,000 in a Roth IRA. You have determined that you are required to withdraw $13,000 to meet the RMD requirement. Further you determined you need to withdraw $26,000 for the current year from your investments to fund your retirement after accounting for other sources of income. The proportional method would suggest withdrawing $5200 from taxable savings ($100,000 divided by $500,000 equals 20% times $26,000 equals $5200). This leaves $20,800 to be withdrawn from your 401k and IRA which more than meets the RMD requirement.

Notice I am not suggesting you touch the Roth IRA because I believe it should contain your most aggressive investments that can grow tax free over the long term. However, using the example above, you could tap the Roth for $3900 ($75,000 divided by $500,000 equals 15% times $26,000 equals $3900). This would reduce the amount needed from your 401K and IRA to $16,900 still meeting the RMD and would reduce your income tax for the current year. The downside is that it could force you to pay a higher tax in later years since you would have a slightly higher RMD to withdraw in the future.

Note that the RMD amount may force you to take out more from your traditional retirement accounts than the proportional amount suggests. Also keep in mind that the amount of your social security income subject to income taxes most likely will increase and therefore raise your total tax. Keeping your withdrawals from accounts subject to RMD's close to the minimum required may make sense, especially if you can draw on other sources without triggering more taxes.

Consider Rolling Over Your 401K

Your employer may allow you to keep your 401K account even after you retire, but should you?

Transferring the money to an IRA in many cases may have the following benefits:

- More investment choices with more asset classes offering greater diversification.

- Lower fees. You may be paying 401K Administrative fees instead of your employer and not realizing it. There could be hidden brokerage costs and other hidden fees you may not be aware of.

- Fewer rules in most cases and your employer can not change the plan like with a 401K.

- The potential to open a Roth account (see Why consider a Roth IRA? below for possible benefits).

- Possible cash incentives from brokers to open an IRA.

- Estate planning advantages. Upon your death, there is a good chance that your 401(k) will be paid in one lump sum to your designated beneficiary. This could cause income and inheritance tax difficulties. It varies depending on your plan, but most companies prefer to distribute the money, so they do not have to maintain the account of an employee who is no longer there. However, inheriting IRA's has regulations too, but IRAs offer more payout options.

If you own company stock either within or outside your 401K, now may be the time to sell some or all of it to better diversify your investments and reduce risk.

The process of rolling over your 401(k) plan is straightforward. First, if you do not have an existing IRA account, open one with a bank, brokerage, or online investing platform. I use both Fidelity and Vanguard because of diversity, low fees, and a great source of retirement information.

Second, you request a direct rollover also called a trustee-to-trustee rollover. Your plan administrator sends the money directly to the IRA account, or they may provide a check made out in the name of your IRA account, which you then send to the IRA account. Make sure the check is not made out to you personally, which will significantly complicate the process to avoid paying income taxes on it. The direct route is the best approach if the administrator will agree. This method is faster, simpler, and there is no doubt that this is not a distribution on which you would owe taxes.

Why consider a Roth IRA? Once you have an IRA account you can open a Roth IRA account if you do not already have one. The following are the Pros and Cons of a Roth IRA:

Pros:

- Roth IRAs offer huge tax advantages, including tax-free growth and tax-free withdrawals in retirement.

- You can withdraw contributions at any time, for any reason, tax-free.

- Unlike traditional IRAs and 401(k), a Roth does not have Required Minimum Distributions.

- Rolling your 401(k) or other retirement plan into a Roth IRA has advantages for high income earners who could not otherwise open a Roth.

Cons:

- You pay tax on the conversion which could be substantial. When you transfer funds from a traditional 401(k) or IRA to a Roth IRA, you will owe taxes on the amount you transfer, and it will be taxed as ordinary income in the tax year you made the transfer. You owe the tax because you received a tax deduction when you made contributions to your 401(k) or traditional IRA. But the Roth is an after-tax option. So, if you roll over contributions made on a pre-tax basis, the amount converted must be included as taxable income for the year in which you made the rollover. If you contributed more than the deductible amount to your 401(k) or IRA, you may be able to avoid immediate taxes by allocating the after-tax funds to a Roth IRA and the pre-tax funds to a traditional IRA.

- You might not benefit if your tax rate will be lower in the future, depending on how much lower, and whether you plan to put riskier investments like stocks and not withdraw from it for 10 or more years. The potential tax-free gains may or may not offset the taxes paid when you converted.

- Rolling over your 401(k) to a new Roth IRA is not a good choice if you anticipate having to withdraw money within five years. Roth IRAs are subject to the five-year rule which states that to withdraw earnings such as interest or profits, you must have held the Roth for at least five years. If not, you must pay a 10% penalty on any money withdrawn from the Roth within five years from the conversion.

A Roth IRA rollover provides the most benefits if:

- *You have the cash to pay the taxes.* You may be tempted to use some of the converted funds to cover your taxes. But that means you will have less in the account, missing out on years of tax-free growth on that money. And, you might owe a 10% penalty for withdrawing it early.

- *It does not trigger significant tax consequences.* Be careful, the amount you convert, when added to your current year's income, could put you into a higher tax bracket or subject you to taxes you otherwise would not pay. For example, retirees who convert from a traditional IRA or 401K to a Roth IRA could end up paying more tax on their Social Security benefits and higher Medicare premiums if the converted amount puts their income above certain levels. A tax advisor can help with this evaluation.

- *Your existing IRA or 401K account has suffered recent losses*. A lower balance in your traditional IRA or 401K means you will owe less tax on the amount converted and have a greater potential for tax-free growth.

- *You are in a lower tax bracket*, due to less income or larger itemized deductions than you normally receive. In this case you could convert just enough to maximize the amount that barely keeps you within the current tax bracket. This is the strategy I use, but you should discuss this with a tax professional.

Converting to a Roth IRA is rather easy, and you can transfer some, or all, of your existing traditional IRA or another tax advantaged account balance to a Roth IRA, regardless of your income. Keep your longer-range retirement goals in mind when deciding to convert to a Roth, and consider these factors:

- Will you be able to afford the taxes due?
- What is your tax rate now, and what will it be in the future?

- When do you need to make withdrawals?

If you do not have a traditional IRA or Roth IRA already, be sure to compare the features of your 401(k) plan with those offered by the IRA's you are considering.

Do You Have an HSA Account?

HSA's have a *Triple Tax Benefit*, in that you did not pay taxes on the money you put in your HSA, you are free to invest it in stocks, bonds, or put it in an interest-bearing savings account, and allow it to grow tax-free.

If you withdraw money from your HSA for something other than *qualified medical expenses* before you turn 65, you must pay income tax plus a 20% penalty. After you turn 65, the 20% penalty goes away.

By using your HSA funds after age 65 for medical expenses, Medicare premiums, or long-term care insurance premiums, you can continue to avoid taxes altogether. You can also use it to pay for qualified medical expenses that Medicare does not cover, such as dental care, eye care, and hearing aids.

Once you reach 65, you can treat your HSA like a traditional IRA if you decide to withdraw money for non-medical retirement expenses. This is certainly an option, but if you have other sources of retirement income, you should probably save your HSA for medical expenses, where you can use it tax-free. Medical costs will most likely continue to become more expensive and they tend to increase with age, so an 85-year-old will generally have significantly more medical expenses than a 65-year-old.

Letting your HSA continue to grow tax-free throughout the early part of your retirement may make a lot of sense. The more you can afford to wait before withdrawing from it, the more you can invest it in higher return investments like bonds or stock mutual funds. The next chapter will look at investing for growth.

Chapter 14

Investing for Growth

This chapter deals with the importance of investing long term to achieve some portfolio growth and to offset inflation. It will first look at dealing with investment risk, then where you should locate your investments, then how they should be allocated for growth, and then keeping those allocations in balance over time.

Avoiding, Managing, or Transferring risk

Avoiding investment risk: Many retirees shy away from holding stocks in their portfolios because they fear losing money in a market downturn. By avoiding stocks, you are trading off one risk for another which is not having enough growth potential to outpace inflation.

Although stocks are often volatile over short periods, they tend to outperform bonds and other conservative investments over long periods. You need to understand that the period of your retirement can be upwards of 30 years, and you will need your savings to support you throughout this entire period. So, while it is important to keep investment risk in check, some allocation to stocks is warranted.

When you avoid investment risk, you generally accept a lower level of potential return in exchange for a potentially higher level of security and stability. You can invest up to $250,000 in an FDIC-insured savings account, but you will need to accept a low interest rate in return. After inflation, you are likely to be losing money, but in seeking a higher return, you need to accept more risk.

Managing Investment Risk: While you are unable to control how the stock market will behave in the future, you may be able to manage the risk of loss by your investment choices. The investment products and accounts you choose can also help limit the taxes and fees you pay.

The following are four common strategies that many financial professionals use to manage risk:

- **Fixed income:** If you are worried about losing money in the stock market, you could consider high quality fixed income products, like Treasury bonds or investment-grade corporate bonds, that provide a fixed rate of return. Keep in mind, investing in bonds is not risk-free and involves several kinds of risk, including default, interest rate, inflation, credit, calling in the bond early, and liquidity risk.

- **Asset allocation:** Stocks historically have provided more return but at more risk than bonds. One important method of managing investment risk is to set a mix of stocks, bonds, and short-term investments that are aligned to your investment time horizon, financial needs, and comfort with volatility.

- **Asset location:** You may be able to reduce federal income taxes by holding highly taxed investments like bonds, stocks held for a year or less, and real estate investment trust funds (REITs), in 401(k)s and IRAs, while leaving investments taxed at relatively low capital gains rates in taxable brokerage accounts. Saving on taxes can help your money grow faster.

- **Tax-smart withdrawals in retirement:** Knowing what accounts you should withdraw from can help you reduce tax liability and make your savings last longer. If you are already retired, consider withdrawing first from your taxable accounts, thereby maximizing the ability of remaining investments to grow tax-efficiently.

Transferring Investment Risk: The insurance industry's existence is built on transferring risk from one form to another. Here are a couple of insurance products to consider:

- **Income annuities:** As covered in detail in chapter 3, if you are concerned about running out of money in your retirement, consider an immediate or deferred income annuity with a lifetime payout option. These annuity contracts are designed to deliver a guaranteed stream of lifetime income beginning immediately or deferred until a date you choose in advance. Be sure to consider fees and work with a financially strong insurance provider. I do not recommend annuitizing more than about 40% of total retirement assets.

- **Long-term care insurance:** This helps you transfer the risk of having to pay for high health care expenses like the cost of nursing homes, which can top $100,000 per year for a private room. The longer you wait to purchase this coverage the more costly premiums become so for those near or in retirement it may be too expensive.

Where to put your investments

Where you put your investments or *asset location* can make a big difference in how much after-tax income you can earn over time. The reason is that different investments and different types of accounts are subject to different tax rules. Sorting your investments into accounts based on their tax efficiency or inefficiency has the potential to both lower your overall tax bill and defer paying taxes for as long as possible.

You may want to consider putting the most tax-efficient investments in taxable accounts and the least tax-efficient in tax-deferred accounts like a traditional IRA, 401(k), deferred annuity, or a tax-exempt account such as a Roth IRA or HSA. The more tax-inefficient an investment is, the more tax you pay on it every year if you hold it in a taxable account.

Tax-inefficient funds generate interest payments that are taxed at ordinary income rates. Individual stocks if bought and held for at least a year are relatively tax-efficient because capital gains on the sale of stocks held for more than a year are currently taxed at federal rates of 0%, 15%, or 20%, depending on income.

In general, the most tax-efficient funds are most Index funds, Tax-managed equity funds, and Municipal bond funds. Value index funds and Small-cap index funds are moderately efficient. The most tax-inefficient funds consist of High-yield bond funds, high turnover active stock funds, and real estate funds (REITs). REITs are tax-inefficient because they are required by law to pay out at least 90% of their taxable income which is generally taxed at higher ordinary income rates. Equity-based exchange-traded funds (ETFs) are like stocks and in most cases are tax-efficient. Large-cap funds have historically tended to be more tax-efficient than similar small-cap funds.

In summary, I would recommend:
- Putting tax efficient investments like stocks, Index funds, ETFs, I-Bonds, and Municipal Bonds in your taxable accounts.

- Putting high growth investments such as stocks and Index funds in a Roth IRA or Roth 401K where they can grow tax free for many years if you can avoid withdrawing them too early.

- Putting tax inefficient investments such as Bonds, Bond funds as well as REITs in your tax deferred accounts like IRAs and 401Ks.

For further information on this approach see Appendix IV References & Resources Chapter 14.

The importance of Asset Allocation

Several groundbreaking studies in the late 1980's and early 1990's including two by Gary P. Brinson, L. Rudolph Hood, and Gilbert L. Beebower, discovered that over 90% of the *variation* in a portfolio's return could be explained by how its funds were allocated among the three major asset classes of stocks, bonds, and cash, *and not by what funds were chosen to be in each asset class*. In other words, **asset allocation has a larger impact on overall portfolio results than the selection of specific securities**.

The findings of these studies have been widely misunderstood. It does not mean that 90% of the *annual rates of return* can be attributed to the allocation of assets, only 90% of the *variability* in returns. The goal of proper asset allocation is to reduce portfolio variability and thus risk.

Since each asset class have different potential average annual gains, along with different variability and their associated risks, these percentages or ratios should change based on your time horizon and how much risk you are willing to accept as you age. The key of course, is to determine what the percent of each asset class should be at any point in time. Cash is not normally considered an investment, so it should be accounted for separately when determining the ratio of stocks and bonds to have.

There are lots of theories and approaches financial planners use and no one-size fits all. John Bogle, founder of Vanguard and author, advises that "as we age, we usually have (1) more wealth to protect, (2) less time to recoup severe losses, (3) greater need for income, and (4) perhaps an increased nervousness as markets jump around. All four of these factors suggest more bonds as we age." He also advocates keeping it simple "Simplicity is the master key to investment success", especially during retirement when you are needing to make withdrawals.

For a relatively conservative low risk investor, he suggests a rule of thumb of subtracting your age from 100 to determine the percentage of stock, and your age in bonds. For a moderately conservative investor, subtracting from 110 would be more appropriate.

As an example, if you are 65 years old and have savings of $500,000 which includes $ 80,000 in cash, it would leave $420,000 to be invested in stocks and bonds. If you are a conservatively low risk investor, you would subtract your age from 100 and have 35% invested in stocks or $147,000 ($420,000 x .35 = $147,000). That would leave $273,000 invested in bonds. Appendix III Table 5A, show various asset allocation ratios and their historical performances.

The Importance of Rebalancing Assets

Once you have chosen your asset mix of stocks, bonds, and cash, I am a strong believer in reviewing the ratios at the beginning of each year, as well as when significant withdrawals are made, or when significant changes in the stock market occur, to see if the ratios have changed enough to trigger rebalancing in order to maintain your target allocation.

The reason is that as stocks rise in a bull market, your stock ratio increases above your target ratio so when it is time to rebalance you would need to reduce your stock holdings, forcing you to sell at high values. Conversely, as stocks fall in a bear market the ratio falls below your target forcing you to buy stocks at lower values. This is also true with bond values.

Following a disciplined rebalancing plan has the added benefit of removing the emotional decisions that occur when investors become brave in a bull market and do not want to miss out. Conversely, when stocks go down investors get scared and want to sell. Buying after large market gains means you are buying at more expensive prices and selling after big market losses means you are selling at cheaper prices. Buying high and selling low is not a particularly good investment strategy.

I strongly suggest you create a document that for each year going forward you list the stock to bond ratios you want to maintain and then at least annually check to see if rebalancing is required. I recommend rebalancing when the ratio itself has moved by 10%, so a 40% stock ratio would be rebalanced if it fell below 36% or if it grew above 44%. I also recommend reviewing and possibly adjusting your target ratios every two years or when a significant life event calls for modifying your risk tolerance.

The importance of reducing investment fees

If you are working with a professional investment advisor, the average fee charged is 1.65 percent and can go as high as 2 percent for a $500,000 portfolio, which is an expensive proposition. Investment fees can really eat into returns for most Americans. According to the U.S. Securities and Exchange Commission, a 1 percent portfolio fee reduces asset values by about $30,000 over 20 years, compared to a portfolio with 0.25 percent in annual fees.

If those fees average 2 percent, investment losses are worse. A Vanguard study showed that regular 2 percent fund management fees would wipe out 40 percent of your portfolio's value. Over a lifetime of investing the amount of fees paid could easily be hundreds of thousands of dollars or more over time. According to Vanguard the biggest predictor of returns are fees, trading costs and taxes.

Check expense ratios. You can look-up your funds online to check the annual expense ratios. A good source is U.S. News which has this information on its mutual fund and ETF fund profiles. It will show what the fund charges on an annual basis. You will not normally see this as a separate fee, as it will be rolled into your total return.

I believe that to reduce costs you must be committed to investigating and questioning your advisors on their strategy and fees. Hidden fees are especially difficult to uncover with most funds. The transaction fees and commissions paid by mutual funds are typically not disclosed.

Consider Index funds. Whether you are doing your own investing or working with an advisor, you can reduce fees and potentially receive higher returns by utilizing a combination of low-cost passive index funds and ETFs, and actively managed funds. For passive funds, the average cost is 0.17 percent, which is much lower than the average 0.75 percent for actively managed funds.

Index funds and exchange-traded funds typically charge a fraction of the fees that most active money managers charge. They also have low turnover in their portfolios keeping costs low. However, while less expensive, these funds are designed to match the performance of the underlying index they emulate and therefor will not outperform the index.

Actively managed funds are managed to beat the indexes and are appropriate for investors who are concerned about losses in a down market since the manager can use strategies to minimize this risk. It is important to pick active managers carefully, choosing those with low fees and good results in both down and up markets, as well as those that keep turnover low (the percent of holdings that are bought and sold each year).

Long-term investors cannot afford to lose up to 40 percent of their portfolio's value to high fees, so it is extremely important that you get educated and keep investment fees to an absolute minimum.

Chapter 15

How will you handle a Major Market Downturn?

How you handle a major market downturn can have major consequences to your retirement lifestyle. The Covid-19 pandemic and resulting market meltdown really tested my own instincts and emotions. Fortunately, many years of investing and living through multiple market cycles taught me many valuable lessons. I thought I would share them.

Do Not Make Major Financial Decisions in a Panic. Your retirement investment strategy requires rational thought and if needed, consulting with a financial planner. The important thing is to stick with your investment plan, while keeping anxiety, and fear out of it. Look to see if there are some expenses that can be delayed or eliminated during bad times. If you created a flexible spending plan it will be easier to accomplish this.

Although it is critical that you adjust your asset allocation, that alone will not protect you from market downturns. When you spend as much as 30 years or more in retirement, you are bound to experience a few recessions that could hurt your overall savings. To protect your retirement lifestyle, plan for how you will get through these recessions. You may need to withdraw less from your retirement fund during these years, and if so, can you afford to get by on less?

Remind yourself that we have come through similar situations in the past. Before panicking, look back into history. The world and markets have been here before, and we will be here again. We always get through it, somehow, some way. As Warren Buffet likes to say, "For 240 years it's been a terrible mistake to bet against America, and now is no time to start."

Doing nothing may be the best strategy even though sometimes, the hardest thing to do is nothing. Remember what your retirement plan goals are. Have those changed? If not, then stay the course and focus on the things you can control. Provided your investment allocations are consistent with your goals, objectives and time horizon, there is no reason to change. You need to give your portfolio the chance to recover.

Do Not try to outthink or time the market. Moving in and out of the market is a losing game over the long run. Like gambling, sometimes you guess correctly, and it will align with what happens because that is how chance works. Make predictions long enough, and eventually a few of them will be right.

When you try to avoid what you perceive as risk by guessing a market downturn, you are taking on *more* risk by trying to time when to jump in or out. One of the biggest costs of market timing is being out of the market when it unexpectedly goes up, potentially missing some of the best performing days.

The opposite of market timing is buying and holding as the markets goes through its cycles. A Merrill Edge study compared investing $1,000 in an S&P 500 index fund. If you did not touch it over the 10-year period from 2009 to 2018 it would have grown to $3,530. However, if you missed only 10 of the best performing months out of 120 it would have grown to only $1,580.

Keep emotions out of it. You should not react with your gut. When emotions run high and markets start to become volatile, a good plan often gets discarded for what feels right in the moment. As John Bogle founder of Vanguard says, "Markets reward discipline and that is why so many investors fail."

Depend on your short-term accounts. In the next chapter I introduce the concept of different buckets of money: a short-term bucket, which is designed to weather short disruptions to your retirement lifestyle, an intermediate bucket designed to weather major disruptions, and a long term bucket to provide enough time for your higher risk investments to grow. When you do not need to sell investments for immediate needs, hopefully you will feel more comfortable staying invested for the long term.

Take a break from checking your account balances too often. It is easy to get alarmed when you see your retirement savings take a large drop in value, but remember that even in retirement, you have a lot of good years left before you would need to withdraw the entire balance. Time is on your side to weather any savings disruptions caused by significant market declines. Historically, market downturns do not last more than a couple of years.

Chapter *16*

Investing for Peace of Mind

Investing invariably involves managing risk. In this chapter we will introduce a method of diversifying your savings and investments for both safety and peace of mind, known as the *Bucket Strategy*. Although there are many versions of this strategy with some versions controversial, I believe a simple bucket strategy has value in considering it.

What is the Bucket Strategy?

The bucket approach to retirement planning is straightforward and makes intuitive sense. The bucket strategy is a system that can provide extra insurance against several years of a down market which can really impact your investments, especially if it occurs early in retirement. Pioneered by Financial Planner Harold Evensky, the Bucket approach is simply a total-return portfolio combined with a cash component (Bucket 1) to meet near-term living expenses and avoid selling under-performing investments that are affected by market swings. The long-term portion of the portfolio is aimed towards maximizing the total return. Money taken from the long-term Bucket is periodically put into Bucket 1 to replenish it to meet living expenses.

Conceptually what makes the "buckets" strategy different from others is that the portfolio is not treated as just one well diversified portfolio but is segregated into separate portfolios or "buckets" each with a different time horizon and risk factor.

In theory, the bucket strategy cannot be superior to a total return strategy because it most likely will hold more cash and less stocks over time, and thus return less growth. However, the trade-off in my opinion is more risk or sleep better at night.

I prefer a simple three-bucket approach which is the system I have used since 2014. The buckets are designed as follows:

Bucket 1: Years 1 thru 3

The goal of this portion of the portfolio is to put funds that have almost no risk of loss to fund near term living expenses. Producing income is secondary so it holds cash instruments and very short duration bonds or bond funds rather than higher yielding but riskier funds with the potential for losses.

This bucket provides both peace of mind and preventing investors from over-reacting to near term market swings thus removing some of the emotion in selling too soon. Investors should look to their expected annual savings withdrawals to determine how much cash should be held in this bucket.

I recommend holding three years of expected withdrawals to fund retirement in this bucket, because three years provides buckets 2 & 3 to have more time to recover from any market downturns. It also provides some flexibility when you need to replenish bucket 1 by selling investments in Bucket 2.

The specific percentage of your savings that bucket one consumes will depend on both the amount of savings you have as well as your spending rate. For example, a retiree with $500,000 in savings who needs to withdraw $20,000 a year to support his or her lifestyle would put 12% of the portfolio in bucket one ($20,000 times three, divided by $500,000). Over time as you age, your time horizon becomes less and depending on how well your investments perform, it could become reduced so that this bucket may hold a larger percentage of cash.

Care must be taken to not hold more cash in this bucket than necessary since it can become a drag on the overall return of your portfolio. You simply earn less money if a larger percentage of your portfolio is held in cash instead of invested in stocks.

Bucket 2: Years 4 thru 10

Bucket 2 is designed to deliver a higher level of income than Bucket 1. Its goal is aimed at inflation protection with some amount of capital appreciation. The reason is that this portion of your savings has a longer time horizon, so inflation protection becomes a concern. Putting I-Bonds and other inflation protected securities that offer inflation protection without the volatility of more risky investments are recommended in this bucket.

I would also recommend short term bond funds for money needing to be withdrawn in years 4 and 5, and intermediate bond funds or bond ladders for years 6 thru 10 as examples of investments that have low risk if held for their duration periods.

Of course, there are many other types of investments that can be held in this bucket, but the emphasis should be on lower risk with some inflation protection and the potential to recover loses within the bucket's time horizon based on historical returns.

Bucket 1 will eventually need to be replenished by selling assets in Bucket 2, and the timing of filling Bucket 1 will depend on how your investments are performing. You would then sell the short duration bonds first.

The specific percentage of your savings that bucket one consumes will again depend on both the amount of savings you have as well as your spending rate. For example, a retiree with $500,000 in savings who needs to withdraw $20,000 a year to support his or her lifestyle would put 28% of the portfolio in bucket two ($20,000 times seven years, divided by $500,000). Over time as you age, your time horizon becomes less and depending on how well your investments perform your portfolio could become reduced so that this bucket will require a larger percentage of conservative to moderate investments.

Bucket 3: Years 11 and Beyond

The long-term portion of your retirement savings contains more risky investments that provide for long-term growth, but also comes with more volatility, so you need a much longer period to recover from any reductions caused by extended bear markets. The theory is that historically since 1926 stocks have only lost value once if held for at least 10 years.

While U.S. large-cap stocks lost money over that decade of 1999 to 2008, cash made money, Bonds made money, International stocks made money, Small caps made money. The key is to have a widely diversified portfolio and not have a high concentration in any one fund like the S&P 500 index fund that did not do well during this period.

When your portfolio of stocks has performed well, and especially when rebalancing each year, you might consider selling your most appreciate stocks as discussed in chapter 13. There may be many years where Bucket 3 does not perform well. It will take discipline to realize it is okay to let Buckets 1 & 2 get to a lower level during these years. There will also be years when your investments perform well, and the buckets can be refilled.

Key Takeaways:

- The bucket strategy is not meant for you to completely reinvent your existing portfolio but to force you to review and possibly rethink your investment strategy and risk tolerance.

- The bucket strategy provides more predictability, confidence, and peace of mind than the traditional total return strategy. It prevents investors from over-reacting to near term market swings, thus removing some of the emotion in selling at the wrong time in the market cycle.

- It provides greater clarity because you can see how each bucket is creating income for each phase of your life.

- Estimating your retirement expenses accurately becomes more important because the bucket strategy works best when investors are staying within their *safe* withdrawal rates such as those determined by using either the 1/N, RMD, or VPW savings withdrawal system.

- It is important to rebalance your investments in conjunction with refilling the buckets to optimize returns over time. It can also help reduce investment risk further. You should not just set-it and forget-it, without carefully managing your investments, or you could find yourself with too risky a portfolio later in retirement if you have allowed your *safe buckets* to be depleted before selling more risky assets such as stocks.

- It helps guard against one of the greatest risks to your retirement which is sequence of returns risk explained in chapter 6.

For more information on the bucket method, see Appendix IV References and Resources Chapter 16.

Chapter 17

How is Your Retirement Plan Doing?

Periodically checking how your retirement plan is doing and tweaking it as you navigate retirement is critical to a successful retirement. I recommend reviewing your plan at least annually, preferably at the beginning of each year to see if your goals, objectives, or life events have change significantly.

It is a good time to evaluate how you are doing in achieving your specific goals. Also check your mix of stocks, bonds, and short-term investments to see if rebalancing may be necessary. You should also evaluate the performance of individual investments against benchmarks. The easiest way to find the appropriate benchmark is on the stock, bond, fund, or ETF research page on Fidelity.com.

Does it still fit into your retirement strategy? Why did you buy this investment? What role is it supposed to play in your overall plan? Ensuring that your mix of investments continues to reflect your chosen level of risk is an important part of the review process. Market moves can shift that allocation out of alignment with your goals. As a result, your investment mix could become more-or-less risky than you intended.

It is also a good time to review your income and spending plan and detailed budget to see how your retirement plan is doing and if any adjustments are needed. I put together the following checklist, which is similar to the one I use, to help remember and check-off all the items that should be reviewed and completed periodically:

Your Checklist

At the Beginning of Every Year:

- If you are using the 4% withdrawal system, take the amount you withdrew last year and increase it by last year's inflation rate. You then add the expected after-tax income for the current year to arrive at your spending budget for the current year.

- For the other withdrawal systems, create the current year Desired Spending Budget (Worksheet 1), Expected After-Tax Annual Income (Worksheet 2), and update the Total Spendable Value of Your Portfolio (Worksheet 3) as of the previous December 31. Also fill out the appropriate withdrawal worksheet you have selected to use each year to determine the suggested withdrawal amount for the current year. I also recommend adding last year's results to the "How Am I Doing" form in Appendix II.

- If you or your spouse have tax differed accounts like IRA's and 401K's (Not Roth IRA's) you may be required by the IRS to withdraw a minimum amount based on your age to avoid a 50% penalty being assessed by the IRS for not withdrawing enough. If you are required to withdraw the RMD, you will need to calculate the amount at the beginning of the year and this amount will be subject to income taxes. You have all year to withdraw it, but I recommend withdrawing as you need it and have the appropriate amount of tax withheld to possibly avoid filing quarterly estimated taxes. You do not have to spend this amount if you withdraw and pay taxes on it. You can save or invest it.

- Once you determine the amount you need to withdraw from your tax differed accounts, you should subtract this amount from the suggested withdrawal amount to determine if you must withdraw more from your savings to meet your spending needs. (See Chapter 13 on which accounts to withdraw from and in what order).

- Now that you know your withdrawal amount for the year, you will need to decide when to withdraw it and which accounts to withdraw from. You will also need to determine if quarterly estimated income tax payments will be required and when to pay them.

- It may also be a good time to check your portfolio to see if further re-balancing is necessary to maintain your target stock, bond, and cash ratios. See Chapters 13 and 14 for further advice.

Mid-Year:

- Review your income and spending budget to see how you are doing and if spending adjustments need to be made.

- Check your emergency fund balance and see if still appropriate.

- Check your reserve fund balance if you have created one and adjust if needed.

Near the End of the Year:

- It is a good time to review how your plan is doing and begin preparing for the beginning of next year when you start the above process over again. You should compare your actual expenditures for the year against the desired spending budget you created at the beginning of the year to see how you did and what changes may be needed in creating your next year budget.

- Unless you are using the 4% withdrawal system, review your emergency fund amount to see if it needs to change before filling out Worksheet 3.

- Ensure that all beneficiary designations on life insurance policies, annuities, and retirement accounts like IRAs and 401(k)s are up to date. Beneficiary designations govern how these assets pass to heirs and they supersede any other directives like a will.

- Review and update your insurance coverage to make sure it still meets your current and future needs.

- Make Sure your Wills and Trusts Are Updated. It is easy to neglect estate planning, and many die every year without an estate plan or one that was not recently updated.

- Where you live plays a huge part in your satisfaction with retirement. And, your home is also probably your biggest expense and most significant asset. Now is a good time to assess whether you are satisfied with where you live and whether it is still a good fit for your finances and desired lifestyle.

Chapter *18*

Summary

I was planning to write a typical summary of key takeaways from each chapter but decided instead to share our retirement plan as an example of what we have learned and tried to incorporate into this book. My wife and I are in our 70's, and like all long-term plans, ours needed to be tweaked along the way. *Keep in mind that our plan may not be a plan that is best for your situation.*

Our retirement plan Highlights:

1. We have chosen to have the portion of our savings that we want to spend in retirement, last through age 95.

2. We have chosen to use the VPW withdrawal system to insure we do not outlive our savings. We believe the VPW system provides us with the best balance between total withdrawals and withdrawal amounts in the early years of retirement versus the latter years. We are comfortable with this approach since we are reasonably healthy, with decent medical insurance, and want to spend more in the earlier years of retirement than the other savings

withdrawal systems allow and are okay with spending lower amounts in the later years.

3. I semi-retired at age 66 because we wanted to save more to fund the retirement lifestyle we wanted to have and was fortunate to have a job that allowed me to slowly cut-back and fully retire at age 71.

4. Delaying retirement also allowed me to delay receiving social security benefits until age 70 and my wife until age 66. This resulted in a significant monthly benefit increase.

5. We took a test drive of our most significant retirement decisions before fully retiring and implementing them.

6. Increased our spending flexibility by reducing the fixed portion of our spending plan. We retired to a warmer climate and to a state with lower taxes while downsizing our housing. At the same time, we were able to increase our retirement happiness.

7. Prior to retiring we were able to pay off the mortgage, recognizing that at our age our investments were not going to return as much as in our younger years when we were willing to take on more investing risk. This of course further reduced our fixed expenses and help reduce the amount of investments at risk.

8. We moved to a secure 55 + gated retirement community and bought a home that was barrier free. We did not want to negotiate stairs as we aged, and we wanted two master bedroom suites so if one of us becomes disabled or needs in-home care we can both be comfortable and age in place for as long as possible.

9. After we fully retired, we downsized to one car since we no longer needed the second car. This also helped to reduce our fixed costs allowing more spending flexibility.

10. We maintain a separate hypothetical reserve fund that acts as a cushion when we need to adjust spending based on how well our investments performed the previous year. (see Chapter 10 for more details).

11. We calculate our RMD amount at the beginning of the year. We also decide how much additional savings we need to withdraw to meet our spending budget for the year. We withdraw the amounts quarterly along with having the appropriate amount of taxes withheld, so that we avoid having to file estimated taxes quarterly.

12. When we need to withdraw money from our portfolio, we choose to sell the most appreciated assets, as outlined in Chapter 13.

13. When we need to withdraw money, we withdraw the amounts proportionately among our taxable and tax deferred accounts to balance our taxes from year-to-year. We do not withdraw from our Roth tax free account, which contains stocks and stock index funds for long term growth beyond 10 years.

14. We use a three-Bucket System for allocating our investments that provides diversification, safety and peace of mind as outlined in Chapter 16. This includes three years' worth of expected future savings withdrawals held in CD's and money market accounts, so we are not forced to sell any of our stocks and bonds too soon. This turned out to be doubly important when the Covid-19 pandemic devasted the stock market.

15. Maintain a 35/50/15 stock to bond to cash ratio since we are both comfortable with this level of risk. Notice I included the percentage of cash since as each year passes, maintaining 3 years of cash requirements becomes a greater percentage of our portfolio. Without cash it would currently be about 40/60 stocks to bonds.

16. Rebalance our portfolio at the beginning of the year, or when significant withdrawal amounts are taken. We try not to let the ratios fall outside a 10% band. So, for a 35% stock ratio we would adjust if below 31% or above 39%. As outlined

in chapter 14, this forces us to sell assets at higher value and buy at lower value.

17. We also review adjusting our target asset ratios every two years or when a significant life event calls for modifying our risk tolerance.

18. We review our retirement plan annually to make sure it is still meeting our needs and goals and adjust if necessary.

19. We rolled over our 401K plan to an IRA as soon as I retired and was no longer getting a contribution from my employer. I was able to reduce fees and have many more options to grow and diversify our investments.

20. I am a strong believer in keeping investment fees to a minimum and only invest in high quality dividend paying stocks and no-load mutual funds especially index mutual stock and bond funds.

21. We currently do not have any annuity contracts, but we do plan to purchase an inflation-indexed Single Premium Immediate Annuity or SPIA near our 80th birthday. It is designed to hedge against one of us living past 95 (eliminating longevity risk) which is the age we used to determine how long we want our savings to last. We plan to buy as much guaranteed income as necessary but not spend more than about 35%

of our remaining portfolio value to purchase it. The SPIA will be structured so that the monthly annuity payment plus all after tax income provides enough income to live comfortably and not be dependent on how well our shrinking portfolio performs.

22. When we buy the SPIA we will cap the VPW savings withdrawal percentage to about 15% since our portfolio will have been reduced by the cost of the SPIA. For more information on this approach see Appendix IV References & Resources Chapters 3, 8, 9, and 17.

CAUTION: What is working for us will not necessarily work for you. Only you can decide which savings withdrawal system and other retirement decisions you are most comfortable with and should only use the results of this book as a guide, not the sole basis of your financial plan. It is recommended that you seek additional guidance in developing a retirement plan you will be most comfortable with.

Appendix I: Estimating Your Income Taxes

Listed are six common types of retirement income that are taxed, and how to estimate your tax rate and total taxes in retirement. The following is for basic general income tax estimation. If you are uncomfortable with estimating your taxes you should consult with a tax professional.

Social Security Income (SSI)

If your only source of retirement income is Social Security, then you probably will not have to pay any taxes in retirement. If you have other sources of income, then a portion of your SSI is likely to be taxed. A rather complicated IRS formula determines the amount of your Social Security that will be taxable. The result is you may have to include as much as 85% of your SSI as taxable income on your tax return.

As a rough example, for the 2019 tax year, a married couple filing jointly, will pay taxes on about 25% of their SSI if their *combined income* is about $47,000. If it is about $57,000, they can expect to pay taxes of about 50% of their SSI and if it is about $70,000 or more 85% will be taxed. The IRS considers *combined income* as including one-half of your SSI, so it does not take much additional income before you start paying taxes on part of your social security income.

The IRS has a worksheet that you can use to determine the exact amount of your SSI that will be taxable.

IRA and 401(k) Withdrawals

Withdrawals from tax-deferred retirement accounts are taxed at ordinary income rates. This means IRA withdrawals as well as withdrawals from 401(k) plans, 403(b) plans, and 457 plans are reported on your tax return as taxable income. Most people will pay some tax when they withdraw money from their IRA or other retirement plans.

The amount of tax you pay depends on the total amount of income and deductions you have and what tax bracket you will be in for that year.

Pensions

Most pension income will be taxable. To determine the likelihood that your pension income will be taxed is if contributions were made before taxes were withheld. If it was, then when you withdraw it, it will be taxable. Most pension accounts are funded with pre-tax income, which means the entire amount of your annual pension income will be included on your tax return as taxable income each year. If your pension is subject to income taxes you can ask that taxes be withheld directly from your pension check.

Annuity Distributions

If your annuity is owned by an IRA or another retirement account, then the tax rules on IRA withdrawals will apply to any withdrawals or annuity payments you receive from that annuity.

If your annuity was purchased with after-tax dollars, then the tax rules that apply depend on what type of annuity you purchased.

Income from an immediate annuity: A portion of each payment you receive from an immediate annuity is considered a return of principal, and a portion is considered interest. Only the interest portion will be included in your taxable income. Each year, the annuity company can tell you how much of the annuity income you receive should be included in your taxable income.

Withdrawals from a fixed or variable annuity: The tax rules on these types of annuities require that earnings be withdrawn first. This means that if your account is worth more than what you contributed to it, when you take withdrawals, you will first be withdrawing earnings or investment gain and it will all be taxable income. Once you have withdrawn all your earnings, you will then be withdrawing your original contributions which are not included in your taxable income because it is considered your cost basis.

Investment Income

You will pay taxes on any dividends, interest income, or capital gains, just as you did before you retired. These types of investment income are reported to you each year on a 1099 tax form, which is sent to you directly from the financial institution that holds your accounts.

If you sell investments that are not inside a retirement account to provide retirement income, each sale will create either a long or short-term capital gain or loss and must be reported on your tax return. If your other income sources are low enough, you may qualify for the 0% capital gains tax rate, which means you would pay no tax on all or a portion of your capital gains for that year.

Gains Upon the Sale of Your Home

If you've lived in your home for at least two years, most likely you will not pay taxes on gains from the sale of your home unless you have gains in excess of $250,000 if single, or $500,000 if married. If you rented out your home, the tax rules get more complicated, and may need to work with a tax professional.

Calculating Your Federal Tax Rate

Your tax rate in retirement will depend on your total amount of income and deductions. To estimate the tax rate, list each type of income and how much will be taxable and determine the total taxable amount. Then reduce that total amount by your expected deductions and exemptions.

For example, assume you are married and file jointly, and you'll have $25,000 of Social Security income, $18,000 a year in pension income, you expect to withdraw $20,000 from your IRA, and you estimate you'll have $3,500 of long-term capital gain income from mutual fund distributions. You add up your ordinary income, but not capital gains and use an estimated 50% of your Social Security benefits. This results in a total of $50,500.

Your standard deduction for 2020 would be $24,800 as a married couple filing jointly. That puts your estimated taxable income at $25,700. You look up the 2020 tax rates and see that puts you in the 12% tax bracket. Since the tax rates are tiered, you will pay 10% on the first $19,750 of taxable income and 12% on the income between $19,750 and $80,250.

In the example above, your estimated tax bill would be $2,689. As you are in the 15% or lower tax bracket for long-term capital gains, your capital gains will qualify for the 0% rate and will not be taxed. Since you will owe more than $1,000 in taxes and to avoid IRS penalties for under-withholding you could either set up quarterly tax payments of $672.25 per quarter, or you could ask your pension to withhold taxes at the 15% rate ($2700) or instead, you could have the IRA withhold 14% ($2800) and receive a small refund.

There are ways to structure your retirement income so that you pay less taxes in retirement. Chapter 13 addresses this in some detail or you may be more comfortable seeking the help of a professional retirement planner or tax advisor.

Calculating Your State Tax Rate

Unless you live in a state that has no state income tax, you will also have to estimate your state income tax. Unfortunately, due to the large number of different tax rules it is not possible to include examples in this exercise.

Appendix II: Keeping Track

Optional but highly recommended that you use the following form to track your progress over time. This will help you see how well your plan is performing and what adjustments you may need to make.

At the beginning of each year record amounts from last years totals						
Year	Estimated Annual Income	Actual Annual Income	Estimated Annual Expenses	Actual Annual Expenses	Portfolio Value at End of Previous Year	Change from Previous Year

Appendix III: Financial Data

TABLE 5A: Historical Financial Data

Time Period	Cash	Stock % / Bond %						
		0/100	20/80	40/60	50/50	60/40	80/20	100/0
40 Years (1979-2018)								
Average annual gain:	4.5%	7.5%	8.6%	9.6%	10.2%	10.7%	11.7%	12.8%
Worst 1 year:	0.1%	-2.9%	-3.2%	-11.7%	-15.9%	-20.1%	-28.6%	-37.0%
Best 1 year:	14.3%	32.7%	30.4%	28.2%	28.0%	29.9%	29.8%	37.6%
% Years Positive:	100%	90%	93%	90%	88%	83%	83%	83%
92 Years (1926-2017)								
Average annual gain:	3.4%	5.4%	6.7%	7.8%	8.4%	8.8%	9.6%	10.3%
Worst 1 year:	0.0%	-8.1%	-10.1%	-18.4%	-22.5%	-26.6%	-34.9%	-43.1%
Best 1 year:	14.3%	32.6%	29.8%	27.9%	32.3%	36.7%	45.4%	54.2%
% Years Positive:	100%	85%	87%	85%	82%	78%	75%	73%

Average Annual Inflation from 1968 to 2017:

30 Years (1988-2017) 2.6%
35 Years (1983-2017) 2.7%
40 Years (1978-2017) 3.6%
45 Years (1973-2017) 4.0%
50 Years (1968-2017) 4.1%

Cash = 3 month T- bills, Bonds = Barclays U.S. Aggregate Bond index or equivalent
Stocks = SP 500 or equivalent
Source: Vanguard, Morningstar, Author

TABLE 5B: Annual Savings Withdrawal Rates Comparison

Years Left	4% System	1/N System	VPW Stock to Bond ratio				RMD System	
			20/80	40/60	60/40	80/20	Age	%
38	3.40%	2.63%	4.00%	4.40%	4.80%	5.20%	62	2.96%
37	3.46%	2.70%	4.00%	4.40%	4.90%	5.30%	63	3.04%
36	3.54%	2.78%	4.10%	4.50%	4.90%	5.30%	64	3.13%
35	3.61%	2.86%	4.20%	4.60%	5.00%	5.40%	65	3.22%
34	3.70%	2.94%	4.30%	4.70%	5.10%	5.50%	66	3.31%
33	3.78%	3.03%	4.40%	4.70%	5.20%	5.60%	67	3.42%
32	3.88%	3.13%	4.50%	4.80%	5.30%	5.60%	68	3.53%
31	3.97%	3.23%	4.60%	4.90%	5.40%	5.70%	69	3.65%
30	4.08%	3.33%	4.70%	5.00%	5.50%	5.80%	70	3.77%
29	4.19%	3.45%	4.80%	5.10%	5.60%	5.90%	71	3.91%
28	4.31%	3.57%	4.90%	5.20%	5.70%	6.00%	72	4.05%
27	4.44%	3.70%	5.00%	5.40%	5.80%	6.10%	73	4.20%
26	4.58%	3.85%	5.10%	5.50%	5.90%	6.30%	74	4.37%
25	4.73%	4.00%	5.30%	5.60%	6.10%	6.40%	75	4.55%
24	4.90%	4.17%	5.50%	5.80%	6.20%	6.50%	76	4.72%
23	5.07%	4.35%	5.60%	6.00%	6.40%	6.70%	77	4.93%
22	5.27%	4.55%	5.80%	6.10%	6.60%	6.90%	78	5.13%
21	5.48%	4.76%	6.00%	6.40%	6.80%	7.10%	79	5.35%
20	5.72%	5.00%	6.30%	6.60%	7.00%	7.30%	80	5.59%
19	5.98%	5.26%	6.50%	6.80%	7.20%	7.50%	81	5.85%
18	6.27%	5.56%	6.80%	7.10%	7.50%	7.80%	82	6.13%
17	6.59%	5.88%	7.10%	7.40%	7.80%	8.10%	83	6.45%
16	6.95%	6.25%	7.50%	7.80%	8.20%	8.50%	84	6.76%
15	7.36%	6.67%	7.90%	8.20%	8.60%	8.90%	85	7.09%
14	7.84%	7.14%	8.30%	8.60%	9.00%	9.30%	86	7.46%
13	8.38%	7.69%	8.90%	9.20%	9.60%	9.80%	87	7.87%
12	9.01%	8.33%	9.50%	9.80%	10.20%	10.40%	88	8.33%
11	9.77%	9.09%	10.30%	10.50%	10.90%	11.20%	89	8.77%
10	10.67%	10.00%	11.10%	11.40%	11.80%	12.00%	90	9.26%
9	11.77%	11.11%	12.20%	12.50%	12.90%	13.10%	91	9.80%
8	13.15%	12.50%	13.60%	13.90%	14.20%	14.50%	92	10.42%
7	14.92%	14.29%	15.40%	15.60%	16.00%	16.20%	93	10.99%
6	17.29%	16.67%	17.70%	18.00%	18.30%	18.50%	94	11.63%
5	20.60%	20.00%	21.00%	21.20%	21.50%	21.80%	95	12.35%
4	25.57%	25.00%	25.90%	26.20%	26.40%	26.60%	96	13.16%
3	33.86%	33.33%	34.20%	34.40%	34.60%	34.80%	97	14.08%
2	50.46%	50.00%	50.60%	50.80%	50.90%	51.10%	98	14.93%
1	100.0%	100.0%	100.0%	100.0%	100.0%	100.0%	99	15.87%

The VPW table is based on a table Collaboratively developed by a group of Bogleheads®. www.bogleheads.org

Appendix IV: References & Resources

Chapters 3, 8, 9 and 17 reference:

For more information regarding the VPW withdrawal system and inflation-indexed Single Premium Immediate Annuity or SPIA, go to **www.bogleheads.org**. It is also a great source for investing and retirement information.

Chapter 12 reference:

www.caniretireyet.com is a good retirement resource. One of the many articles on the site discusses the importance of where you should withdraw your money from based on stock and bond market performance to maximize your investment gains over time. See the article "The Best Retirement Withdrawal Strategies: Digging Deeper" by Darrow Kirkpatrick.

Chapter 13 reference:

"Determinants of Portfolio Performance" by Gary P. Brinson,
L. Rudolph Hood, and Gilbert L. Beebower

Chapter 15 reference:

www.morningstar.com Christine Benz has several good articles on the basics of setting up and maintaining a "Bucket" retirement portfolio, including some of her favorite funds for retirees.

Additional Resources:

1. **www.Vanguard.com** and **www.Fidelity.com** are excellent resources regarding retirement planning.

2. "Common Sense on Mutual Funds" John C. Bogle founder of Vanguard

3. "How much can I spend in retirement? A guide to investment-based retirement income strategies" a book written by Wade Pfau Ph.D., CFA is an excellent reference book although quite lengthy with lots of detail.

4. "The Bogleheads' Guide to Retirement Planning" a book by Taylor Larimore, Mel Lindauer, Richard A. Ferri, and Laura F. Dogu

5. "The Bogleheads Guide to Investing" a book by Taylor Larimore, Mel Lindauer, and Michael LeBoeuf

6. "The 4% Rule Safe Withdrawal rates in Retirement" a book by Todd Tresidder

7. "Asset Dedication: How to grow Wealthy with The Next Generation of Asset Allocation" a book by Stephen J. Huxley and J. Brent Burns

Afterword

The free companion spreadsheet to this book is available both as a Microsoft Excel .xlsx and as a LibreOffice .ods file. To receive it, send me an email at **retirementdilemma@outlook.com** and let me know which version you want.

If you would prefer to receive printable copies of the worksheets to fill in manually each year, send me an email request for the Worksheets pdf file.

If this book helped you answer the questions raised at the beginning of the book and that it was worth reading, please let others know by providing a review at **www.amazon.com**. Search on my book title or my name then scroll down until you see "Write a Customer Review" and click on it. Reviews truly matter in helping others discover my book and I read every one of them.

If you were not satisfied, or you have suggestions for making this book better, please let me know and I promise I will respond.

Thank you for purchasing this book.

www.ingramcontent.com/pod-product-compliance
Lightning Source LLC
Chambersburg PA
CBHW071357210526
45465CB00001B/133